THE PRISONERS, 1914–18

ROBERT JACKSON

ROUTLEDGE
LONDON AND NEW YORK

First published 1989
by Routledge
11 New Fetter Lane, London EC4P 4EE
29 West 35th Street, New York, NY 10001

Typeset in 10/12pt Baskerville Linotron 202
by Hope Services, Abingdon
Printed in Great Britain
by Biddles Ltd, Guildford

British Library Cataloguing in Publication Data
Jackson, Robert, *1941–*
The prisoners 1914–18.
1. Germany. British prisoners of war, 1914–
1918 – Biographies – Collections
I. Title
940.4'72'430922
ISBN 0–415–03377–2

Library of Congress Cataloging in Publication Data
also available

CONTENTS

ILLUSTRATIONS

(*Between pp. 76 and 77*)

1 Donington Hall, near Derby – the former ancestral home of the Hastings family – was used as a POW camp for German naval and military officers during the 1914–18 War. Kapitänleutnant Gunther Plüschow succeeded in escaping from here in July 1915 and stowed away on a ship bound for Holland.

2 Kapitän Maerker, the captain of *HIMS Gneisenau* – sunk during the Battle of the Falkland Islands in December 1914 – was an early inmate of Donington Hall.

3 German prisoners being escorted to an assembly area during the Battle of Flers-Courcelette, September 1916.

4 A captured German machine-gun crew pictured during the savage fighting around Arras, April 1917.

5 Civilian internees making their way to Ruhleben Camp in 1914. The men appear cheerful enough, doubtless believing that it would 'all be over by Christmas'. Four years of harsh reality lay ahead of them.

6 Prisoners queueing up for their rations at Ruhleben.

7 Scorning the poor facilities provided by the Germans, the internees in Ruhleben set up their own businesses and entertainments. Here, a group of internees looks forward to a performance at the 'Ruhleben Empire'.

8 A boxing match in progress at Ruhleben. Entertainments such as this played a vital part in sustaining morale, which remained generally good.

9 British, French and German walking wounded receiving treatment at a casualty clearing station during the Battle of the Lys, April 1918.

ACKNOWLEDGEMENTS

In the preparation of this book I have received enormous help from Roderick Suddaby, Keeper of Documents at the Imperial War Museum, London, and indeed all the staff in the Department of Documents. For their efficiency and willingness to help I am deeply grateful.

Chapter 1

THE RULES OF WAR

The 25th of December, 1914, was not a particularly significant day in the diary of a war which, contrary to many predictions, had now been in progress for 136 days and which showed no sign of ending. On this day Field Marshal Sir John French, commander of the British Expeditionary Force, announced that two British armies – the First Army under General Haig and the Second Army under General Smith-Dorrien – were to be formed on the western front; in the North Sea the Royal Navy was reinforcing its battle squadrons in anticipation of a major engagement with the Imperial German Navy; British naval aircraft and submarines were skirmishing with enemy warships off Cuxhaven; a German aircraft had appeared over Sheerness; and on some sectors of the front, German and Allied troops were holding an unscheduled truce, meeting in no man's land to exchange food and tobacco and, in places, to kick a football around.

On the eastern front there was no truce. Here, a German drive on Warsaw had been stopped; the Russians, recovering after a series of crushing defeats earlier in the year, had retaken the Lupkov and Dukla Passes in the Carpathians from the Austro-Hungarians, and defeated the Austrians at Tarnov in Galicia.

And in the prisoner-of-war camp at Wittenberg, thirty miles south-west of Berlin, men were beginning to die.

The Wittenberg camp was built on a flat, sandy plain and covered an area of ten and a half acres, surrounded by a double fence of barbed wire. As many as sixteen thousand prisoners were housed in hastily erected wooden huts. Most of them were Russians, the remnants of three Russian army corps destroyed at Tannenberg in August 1914 and of other Russian formations mauled at Lodz in the early winter. One hundred thousand prisoners had been taken at Tannenberg alone, a number so vast that the Germans had no machinery to deal with their needs. Already hungry and ill-clad when the battle was joined, many had succumbed to starvation, sickness, and exhaustion in the days that followed, as the ragged columns marched westward to makeshift prison camps in eastern Germany.

The Mark of Brandenburg, in which Berlin and the towns near by are situated, can be a pitiless place in winter. The only wind-break between this region of central Europe and Siberia are the Ural Mountains, while the nearest sea, the Baltic, is not blessed by the Gulf Stream and much of it usually freezes over. When the particularly severe winter of 1914–15 descended on Wittenberg, it set the scene for a catastrophe.

The prisoners' daily rations at Wittenberg consisted of a one-kilogram loaf of black bread between ten men, with a thin soup made from potato flour and horse beans. Meat was non-existent. The heating arrangements in the barrack huts were hopelessly inadequate; there were stoves, but these were so small that they had to be filled to their maximum capacity and kept constantly stoked to produce anywhere near an acceptable degree of heat – an impossibility, for fuel was in short supply. There was only one mattress for every three men, who took it in turns to use it, and blankets were mostly used as clothing. The Russians received no parcels from home to supplement their starvation diet; it was little wonder that Major Priestley, who was one of the medical officers involved, described them as 'gaunt, of a peculiar grey pallor, and verminous'.

When the typhus epidemic broke out, it spread like wildfire through the crowded camp. The German reaction was to withdraw their guards and medical orderlies to a place of safety on the other side of the wire. It was not until February 1915, nearly two months after the outbreak, that six captured British medical officers were sent to Wittenberg to try to help the unfortunate inmates. These officers – Majors Fry and Priestley, with Captains Sutcliffe, Field, Vidal, and Lauder – were appalled by the conditions they found there. No attempt had been made to segregate typhus sufferers from the other prisoners. Typhus patients were being given a 'special diet' consisting of an extra slice of bread and half a cup of milk per day. There was no special hospital clothing for them, they had no extra blankets, and all were heavily infested. Satisfactory washing arrangements were out of the question, for there was no soap and very little hot water. Some patients were moved to two hospitals outside the camp, where conditions were a little better, but they represented only a small proportion of the total cases.

The British medical officers did their utmost to bring about a degree of order, and to an extent succeeded. Only then did the German medical officer who was responsible for Wittenberg, one Dr Aschenbach – who had been conspicuously absent from both the POW camp and the hospitals since the outbreak of the epidemic – agree to return. Even then he came for only one brief tour of inspection, dressed in a full suit of protective clothing, complete with mask and rubber gloves.

Shortly after this, Major Priestley and Captain Vidal were sent to work in the hospitals outside the camp. When they returned, it was to find that Major Fry and Captain Sutcliffe were dying of typhus. Captain Field and Captain Lauder also contracted the disease; Field died, but Lauder somehow continued to work and recovered.

A subsequent report by a British investigating committee on the conditions on Wittenberg told how

> Some of the German guards outside the camp were infected by prisoners to whom, contrary to orders, they persisted in selling things. These men were placed by the Germans in a hospital outside the camp, and one of the German medical staff, an Alsatian as it happened, was sent to attend them. At a later stage in the outbreak this young man came to the hospital, but simply to take bacteriological specimens for research work at Magdeburg. He helped in no way. With these exceptions no visit was paid to the camp during the whole outbreak by any member of the German medical service. The dead were buried in a cemetery formed out of a part of the camp. The Germans sent in a certain number of coffins every day, into which the bodies of the dead were put and carried out by their comrades through a gate in the barbed wire. There was not sufficient room for burial of so many, and the coffins were piled one upon another.

It was not until April 1915 that bedding, clothing, and medical supplies were available in any quantity. With the advent of warmer weather the cases began to decrease in number, but it was to be several months before the disease was eradicated completely at

Wittenberg, and even so this gradual improvement was only due to the tireless work of the surviving British medical officers.

The terrible events at Wittenberg are recounted here not as an indictment of conditions in a typical German POW camp in the early part of the 1914–18 war, because in reality they were far from typical, but to stress the almost total inadequacy and unprepared-ness of the German prisoner-of-war system. The Germans were not at fault alone; amazingly, none of the belligerent nations had given much thought, prior to the outbreak of war, to the logistical problems involved in handling and sustaining large numbers of prisoners, although the rules governing their treatment had long since been formulated.

The plight of military prisoners had aroused repeated concern among various parties and individuals, if not governments, during the wars of the nineteenth century, but it was left to the embryo Red Cross organization to work out a firm code of practice. In 1864, Henri Dunant, a Swiss citizen who had founded the International Committee of the Red Cross after witnessing the misery of wounded French and Austrian soldiers at the Battle of Solferino in June 1859, arranged the first Geneva Convention with the help of a number of dedicated colleagues. The object of the convention, which was attended by delegates of the leading powers, was to discuss ways of improving the condition of wounded soldiers. There was no mention at this stage of how prisoners were to be treated beyond their immediate care on the battlefield, but it was the start of a process which was to gain momentum, albeit slowly, over the next half-century. A second step in the right direction was taken in 1870, when the International Committee of the Red Cross established an office in Basle and set up a department specifically to deal with soldiers listed as wounded and missing.

During the Franco-Prussian War, this department, and a subsidiary office set up in Berlin, answered some 60,000 inquiries about missing French personnel, and handled 186,000 letters to and from French prisoners of war. Apart from this, however, the department did not actively seek to promote the welfare of military prisoners; indeed, with a staff of fewer than thirty people it is difficult to see how it could have done so. The work of the Red Cross bureaux had nevertheless made its mark, and in 1899 the international delegates to another conference, held this time at The Hague, recommended their expansion. This first Hague Conference also saw the evolution of the *Regulations respecting the Laws and Customs of War*, which laid the foundations for a code of conduct between belligerents. Regarding the status of a prisoner of war, the principal clauses in the Hague Rules, amended at a second Hague Conference of 1907, stipulated that:

1 He is the captive of the government of the enemy country and not of the individual who captured him.
2 He must be protected by his captors from violence, insults, and public curiosity.
3 When interrogated, he is obliged to reveal only his name and rank; and no pressure may be brought to bear to force him to give any other information.
4 His permanent place of captivity must not be in a district which is unhealthy, nor in an area where he will be exposed to the fire of the fighting zone. He may be reasonably restrained but he must not be strictly confined except under absolute necessity.
5 He must be given freedom of religious worship.
6 He must be treated with due regard to his rank and age. If he is an officer he cannot be obliged to work, and, if an NCO, can be obliged to work only in a supervisory capacity. A working prisoner must not be made to work longer hours than a soldier of his captors' army and must be paid the same rate of wages. He cannot be required to do work which is directly concerned with the captors' war effort.
7 He must be allowed to correspond with home and to receive parcels of food, clothing, and books.
8 Attempts to escape shall be punished only by disciplinary action – usually a spell of solitary confinement. All forms of corporal punishment, confinement in cells not illuminated by daylight, and all other forms of cruelty whatsoever are prohibited as disciplinary punishment; nor may the prisoner be deprived of his rank.

In reality these were guidelines, and nothing more; there were many loopholes and omissions, and the clauses themselves were open to different interpretations. Nevertheless, the so-called Hague Rules were infinitely better than anything that had existed before, and when they were written into the *British Manual of Military Law* and its German equivalent, the *Kriegsbrauch* ('war usage'), the interpretations placed upon them were often remarkably similar. For example, both agreed that the right of interrogation was not restricted to name and rank, although a prisoner was not bound to reply to other questions. It was permissible to employ every means, provided they were humane and not compulsive, to obtain all possible information from prisoners with regard to the numbers, movements, and location of the enemy. A prisoner could not be punished for giving false information about his own army. The German version went a stage further in stating that to shoot a prisoner for giving false information would be 'cowardly murder', but that it would be in order to execute a requisitioned civilian guide who deliberately misled the troops.

As far as food was concerned, the Hague Rules stipulated that a prisoner was to receive the same rations as the troops of the government which captured him. This was vague, and most of the signatories, including Britain and Germany, took it to mean that a prisoner was to be fed on the same scale as peacetime depot troops, with no extras. The British realized that there might be a huge variation in the diet to which a prisoner was accustomed and that of a soldier of the army which captured him, and made allowances for this in the *Manual*; they were the only nation to do so.

The Hague Rules expressly forbade the killing of enemy soldiers who had surrendered and who were defenceless, having laid down their arms. The *British Manual* approached this topic with some caution:

> A commander may not put his prisoners to death because their presence retards his movements or diminishes his means of resistance by necessitating a large guard, or by reason of their consuming his supplies, or because it appears certain that they will regain their liberty through an impending success of their own army. Whether nowadays such extreme necessity can ever arise as will compel a commander on grounds of self-preservation to kill his prisoners may well be doubted.

The German *Kriegsbrauch* showed less restraint:

> Prisoners can be killed . . . in cases of extreme necessity when other means of security are not available and the presence of prisoners is a danger to one's own existence. . . . Exigencies of war and the safety of the State come first and not the consideration that prisoners of war must at any cost remain unmolested.

There is no doubt that prisoners of war were shot by all the belligerents during the 1914–18 war, but this usually occurred as a result of individual acts of violence soon after capture. There is no evidence to support any claim that prisoners were murdered as the result of orders issued by higher authority, although civilian captives were executed by the German Army in the occupied territories. It was a universally recognized rule of international law that hostilities were restricted to the armed forces of the belligerents, and that ordinary citizens of the contending States must be treated leniently and must not be deprived of their lives or liberty; this understanding, however, excluded those who took up arms and committed what were deemed to be hostile acts against enemy forces.

This exclusion gave the Germans *carte blanche* to act with great ferocity during the first days of the war, when invading German troops came into conflict, albeit under very confused circumstances, with Belgian civilians. In a series of violent reprisals the Germans shot several hundred Belgian townspeople in Andenne, Tammines, Dinant, and Louvain, announcing to the world the *Schrecklichkeit* ('frightfulness') of which the 'Hun' was capable. The stories of the executions were true, but those of the rape and torture which accompanied them were not. During the months that followed, propaganda piled atrocity after atrocity on the heads of the Kaiser's armies; thousands of Allied soldiers went to war fully believing that 'frightfulness' was all they might expect if they were captured, and when it happened were astonished to find that the rapacious Huns were, for the most part, a mixture of ordinary men much like themselves, preoccupied with food and survival.

Prisoners were, in the natural course of events, to experience hardships at the hands of brutal guards and camp commandants, and the Germans by no means had a monopoly on these. Once again, propaganda was to seize on such stories and make great revelations out of them. Sadly, the propaganda machine was believed by most of those at whom its outpourings were directed; and, on both sides, men behind barbed-wire were to suffer because of it.

Chapter 2

CAPTURE AND TREATMENT

The initial German successes on the western front during the last week of August 1914 brought them their first major haul of British prisoners. During the battle of Le Cateau, on 26 August, many British units were cut off by the rapid enemy advance; of the 2,000 or so troops who found themselves stranded in enemy territory about a third managed to fight their way out of the trap, but the rest, many of them wounded, had no alternative but to surrender. They soon discovered that the Germans had little or no organization with which to cope with an unexpectedly large number of POWs.

One of these early prisoners was Corporal John Brady of the King's Own Yorkshire Light Infantry, who was wounded, although not seriously, and captured at Le Cateau at 5.30 p.m. on 26 August. Together with other prisoners, he was penned into a church, his wounds untended until the following morning. Afterwards, the prisoners were marched to the rear and spent their second night of captivity in another church; in the morning they received their first food, a small issue of black bread. Marching on to Mons, they were issued with a loaf of bread between ten men that evening; the meagre ration worked out at one slice per man. The next morning they received six potatoes per man, which they roasted in small fires which their captors allowed them to build; they were also given some boiled potatoes by sympathetic French prisoners. It was to be their last food for two days and nights; they were crammed into a train at Hal, eighteen men in compartments designed to seat eight, and set off into Germany, destination unknown.

Apart from the shortage of food, Brady and the others were not treated badly. This was also the experience of an anonymous NCO of the 1st Battalion of the Hampshire Regiment, in action near Beaucourt on 27 August:

> Here it was I was wounded. Fragments of a shell struck my right arm and abdomen, also my right leg, and I was unable to walk, and Captain F. C. Moore, who was with me when I was hit and who helped me out of the firing line, ordered me to be taken to a small wayside hospital at Ligny. I reached the hospital at about 4 p.m.; the village of Ligny was then being shelled. Later in the evening I asked the MO for permission to leave hospital to try and get away to avoid being captured, but this he refused me. Next morning the hospital was taken over by the Germans, and the wounded were made prisoners. . . . We all remained in the hospital for that day, and the following morning those who were able to be moved were put into French wagons which the Germans had commandeered, and sent into Germany.
>
> At Ligny we came across German reinforcements which were being hurried into the line, and they treated us with little courtesy. The German officer in charge of us, who spoke English well, spoke kindly to us and told us to take no notice as they had as yet done no fighting, and when they had, their tale would be different.

It was not necessarily so, as Corporal C. E. Green of the 1st Battalion of the Scots Guards learned a few weeks later, in action at Ghelnvelt during the last days of October 1914. His diary tells the story:

> 29.10.14. At dawn Germans made heavy attack, but were repulsed, leaving hundreds of dead and wounded on the field. Received news the enemy had broken through on our right, and were round us. About 11 a.m. they came on to us, and we were made prisoners. About 200 all told. After a search they marched us off to Belselair. I shall never forget the search and the ensuing few hours. The ever-gallant Huns made us go on knees, and proceeded to take our money, tobacco, cigarettes, etc. from us and make away with them. As luck would have it, the searchers gave me back my tobacco and pipes. Some fellows, who had previously obtained money from dead Huns, were very roughly handled.
>
> The soldiers in charge of us insisted on us marching with our

arms over heads. At the end of an hour, we halted for a rest. Just before this halt, we had stopped at a farm house, where the wounded were attended to. Again proceeding, we passed many German soldiers, who made signs as if they would like to cut our throats. Eventually we arrived at the German headquarters in Belselair, four or five miles distant. For an hour or so they kept us in a church. . . . About 4 p.m. they packed us into trains, and an hour and a half later we arrived in Courtrai, where the enemy were then concentrating their army. We were then packed into cattle trucks very tightly. The next morning on getting up from a very hard bed, we were given a slice of black bread, but nothing to drink.

30.10.14. Later on in the day our train halted again, and we enquired for a drink of water. A man duly went away, returning with a bucketful. But instead of receiving it to drink, he threw it in our faces. . . .

31.10.14. We had nothing to eat since the previous day, although many halts had been made. However, about 3 a.m. we were ordered from the train and given a big black loaf between six men, which puzzled us as we had no sharp instrument to cut it with. However, by means of a little piece of tin, it was done. Soon after restarting we passed the ruined town of Louvain, once a beautiful and picturesque place. About 8 p.m. we again stopped and were marched into a large wooden hut, receiving some barley soup and specimens of sausage.

1.11.14. Another halt, some soup and a thin slice of bread. We then marched to the latrines, and we were compelled to run back, or if not they gave us a rifle butt in the ribs or an inch of bayonet. At 7 p.m. another halt, and feed of coffee, bread and raw bacon, eaten as though it was the finest cooked. This was the last food we had on the train.

Any assertion that officer prisoners were invariably better treated than other ranks is ill-founded; treatment depended entirely on the circumstances of the capture and the calibre of the enemy troops who happened to be in the vicinity at the time. Special treatment was certainly not accorded to Lieutenant William Cecil Blain, Royal Flying Corps, and his observer when their Be.2C army co-operation

10

aircraft was forced to land behind the enemy lines as a result of engine failure on 7 August 1916.

We were at once surrounded by a crowd of unfortunate French peasants, who in vain tried to persuade us to get up in the air once again, that we had landed on the wrong side – the treatment was very bad, etc., etc. However, having shaken hands with most of them, and told them very briefly that we were winning and that it might be over next year, we set to work to put the old machine to nought. This we did by putting fists, feet, etc., through the fabric of the planes, and then applying matches. It burnt well, the petrol tank burst as the Huns arrived, and the heat caused the cartridges in the Vickers-belt to explode at an alarming rate, thus in all probability putting quite a good finishing touch to the engine.

We were searched there and then and marched off along the road. As soon as we got to the nearest village a German officer arrived in a large car, took us on board and thence to the nearest Post-office. Here he took all our letters and money and asked a few questions. He spoke fairly good English, but we managed to keep our mouths fairly well closed by informing him that we did not understand. He then took us to the Citadel of Cambrai – quite an old-fashioned place, with a moat, drawbridge and a high wall all around.

It was here that we gained our first impression of the treatment behind the lines. We spent about eleven days here in this place under the most foul conditions. We were put into a small room by ourselves and not allowed to speak to anyone. In the room there were two beds and mattresses, and on each bed two blankets which, judging by the smell and grease on each, might have been used for the same purpose in the last French war.

I cannot here relate all the details of this place. The heat was intense and the smells almost unbearable, which enticed flies and other vile insects by the million. The place was fairly full. Dysentery raged among the men, and as far as I could judge no attempt to check it was made. The wounded were practically uncared for, and it was not an uncommon sight to see an English soldier looking like death, holding up an arm which was a mass of blood, straw, dirt and raw flesh! I heard that the reason given for this was that all minor wounds were left for three days, because at the end of that time they (the Hun doctors) would know whether the wound was a dirty one or not!

For the first day we were not allowed food at all, and our first meal on the following morning was a hunk of the sourest black bread, and imitation coffee. We were hungry, but we could not finish the bread. At noon we had some barley soup made of any kind of vegetable they could lay their hands on – mostly turnips. This mush was given to us all in the different sorts of bedroom utensils, basins, slop-pails, etc. . . . On the morning of the second day we were taken to Headquarters to be questioned. Nothing much came of this except that we found out for certain about the death of some of our friends a few days previous. We were then taken to Bapaume aerodrome where we were allowed to climb over most of their machines, while the Huns cunningly tried to make us compare notes on various gadgets on their machines which we might have had on our own. I don't think by their remarks to us that they were very successful. We returned to our hole for food and stayed there without any further amusement of this sort.

At length the time came for us to be shifted, and with a batch of newly captured infantry officers we boarded a train for Germany. We made some futile plans for escaping on the way but nothing came of them. At various intervals we were inflated with bean soup, and on one occasion, by paying for it, we managed to get quite a reasonable feed of meat and vegetables at a railway station. We were also able to buy chocolate at this place.

After about three days' travelling, we arrived at our first camp in Germany, Gütersloh. We were at once put into quarantine and treated for our bad 'itchings' and other ailments.

In some cases, there was a sharp contrast between the treatment of officers on capture and their subsequent experiences in the cells, pending transfer to a POW camp. This is apparent in the account of Captain H. Champion of the RFC, who was shot down on 28 February 1916; he and his observer escaped unhurt and were treated with impeccable courtesy, although his account reveals an underlying theme of very subtle interrogation.

It wasn't long before we were conducted to a car and driven to Wegelhem, the HQ of the 13th Army Corps. The streets were filled with people, several women wept at seeing us, others merely stood with open mouths, others waved, clearly we had their sympathy. We were taken in a car to what I presume was the HQ and put in a half basement room with a window on to the pavement. It was an office of sorts and occupied by a distinguished looking old gentleman, who offered us cigarettes and wine. This at 9 a.m. was more than hospitality. The former we took and found them excellent. Our escort withdrew and we were left alone with the old gentleman and a Uhlan to guard us. . . .

The old gentleman was most affable. He informed me that he was a son or brother or some relation of the King of Württemberg, but I was unable to understand the exact relationship. . . . After about an hour an interpreter and several officers arrived, amongst them the Archie merchant from the Ypres–Menin Road [the officer in charge of the AA battery which had fired on Champion's aircraft]. The interpreter began by asking where we came from, our army, our corps, etc. I at once explained that the only information necessary was my name and rank, our regiments were obvious. [RFC officers continued to wear the insignia of the regiment in which they had served prior to their transfer to the flying service.] He continued to explain the positions and numbers of our squadrons, also the names of our squadron commanders, his information was most accurate, but we were careful not to contradict any errors, or agree with any facts.

He then told us that two other machines had been brought down, which we afterwards discovered to be untrue. He stated that the Archie officer claimed to have brought us down. I denied it, and he explained my denial to the officer concerned who became very cross, much to the amusement of the others. He then asked the interpreter to question me as to the position of his bursts. I understood his meaning, and before the interpreter spoke I explained that I refused to give this information. 'So you speak German,' said the interpreter. I explained that I did not, and only managed to understand a little probably more by his gestures than his words. I was unbelieved and suspected of this crime for the rest of my sojourn wherever I went. I turned round and found Newbold busily engaged talking to a pilot no bigger than himself. This was one of our friends that we had met above some few hours before. He could say very little more than 'Souvenir' and was very keen on Newbold's cap badge. . . .

The cross-questioning had ended, and everyone was talking at once. It was most interesting. It was explained that if we wished to send a note to our Squadrons we could do so, and it would be dropped over the lines. We each wrote a note simply saying that we were unwounded and wished our Squadron the best of luck. We were careful to give no number or mention any names. . . . Whether these notes were ever dropped or were lost it was impossible to say, but they were never delivered to HQ.

The crowd gradually withdrew, and after a short interval two officers came in and we were taken to the 'Casino' or Staff Mess. We were shown into the ante-room and introduced to a Captain who spoke excellent English. We were treated as guests. We were asked if we wished to have a wash, and readily accepted. We were shown to the lavatory and left alone. Newbold was carrying his pass, and quickly destroyed it. Luckily we had not been searched. I also destroyed one or two letters I had on me.

We went back to the ante-room, and were offered a cocktail and cigarettes. The Captain was most interesting, and discussed the difficulties of German espionage in our lines as the population was hostile, whereas our agents were acting in a country where the population was friendly. Officers began to arrive and they all saluted with a click of the heels and a bow on entering. They all seemed to treat our host with the greatest respect. The conversation led on to the use of poison gas [which was then in its infancy]. He stated amid a deep silence, 'I think it is perfectly disgusting.' My heart went out to this man, he was at least a sportsman.

We sat down to lunch and discussed Verdun. They had hope of its fall at any moment. . . . Lunch finished our host explained that he had to visit the trenches that afternoon, as he was MG Officer to the Corps. He bade us farewell, and I wished him the best of luck. We were escorted back to the old gentleman. It was then explained that our host was a Coburg, and a cousin of our King. I believe that he was educated at Eton.

It was all very Boys' Own Paper-ish, but the illusion was not to last. Champion and Newbold returned from the mess to find that their coats had been rifled and everything taken from the pockets. They were then marched seven miles to Courtrai where they were locked in separate cells. These

14

measured twelve foot by six foot, the furniture consisted of a stretcher covered with a filthy mattress, a chair and a basin in the corner. Light and air was admitted by a small barred window about seven foot from the floor. . . . I prepared to sleep and covered the bed with my leather coat. The smell of humanity in the cell was nauseating. The basin had not been emptied for days. It was not long before I discovered that I was not the only occupant of the cell. Their numbers were legion, and of three distinct species.

It was bitterly cold and the window simply had to be left open. The condition of that cell was almost beyond description. The night seemed endless. I was in agony with cold, fatigue and constant irritation.

Champion and Newbold had, in fact, been thrown into the town jail, which was mostly filled with civilians under sentence of death for some capital offence against the Germans. They were later taken, via Brussels, to Cologne, where they were imprisoned in a twenty-foot-square cell under the platform, known to other British servicemen who had passed that way as the 'Black Hole of Cologne', before the final stage of their journey to prison camp at Mainz.

Captives of the Imperial German Navy, whether officers or ratings, were almost always treated exceptionally well while they remained in Navy hands. In April 1917, Captain Norman Lewis, RN, was in command of the 'Q' ship Q.12 – the sloop HMS *Tulip*, modified to resemble a merchant vessel and heavily armed for the purpose of engaging surfaced U-boats – when she was torpedoed by one of them, the U-62. The sixty survivors and the captain were taken aboard the surfaced submarine.

My crew in their disguises as merchant seamen looked a sorry enough collection, in dirty clothes, rakish caps and with unshaven chins, but none presented such a disreputable appearance as myself, the 'skipper' – collarless, tieless, coatless and hatless, wearing only a grimy jersey, a pair of old blue trousers and slippers – and it was with shamefaced reluctance that I admitted to being the captain of the ill-fated vessel.

However, I was taken aboard after bidding farewell to my men in the boats and led down through the conning-tower and into the presence of the captain – Captain Ernst Hashagen. I began to wonder what my fate would be as I faced this tall, clean-shaven, pleasant-looking officer with the Iron Cross. One was well aware in those days that the operations of 'Q' ships were proving a very painful thorn in the flesh of the Germans, and that little mercy had been shown to the personnel of 'Q' ships on those few occasions recently when they had fallen into the hands of the enemy. [This was supposition rather than fact.]

Lewis was very surprised when the U-boat commander asked him to have a drink. Afterwards, Lewis was allowed on deck to bid farewell to his crew; Hashagen asked them if they had sufficient provisions to last them until they were picked up, was assured that they had, and then ordered the submarine to draw away. In fact, the crew were picked up the next day by a British destroyer.

Lewis spent nineteen days aboard the U-62 while the submarine cruised off the Irish and English coasts, sinking an average of one vessel each day. Although the experience was harrowing – the U-62 was subjected to a severe depth-charging on one occasion – he had nothing but praise for her captain and crew.

> The treatment I received aboard U-62 during my involuntary three weeks' undersea trip was irreproachable. Nothing but kindness was meted out to me by men and officers alike. The doctor lent me his fur coat to cover my shabby garb; the officers lavished cigarettes on me. I dined with the officers, and they pressed wine and liqueurs on me. Captain Hashagen, who was one of the aces of the German U-boat service, behaved in the friendliest possible manner.
>
> U-62 returned to Wilhelmshaven via the west coast of Scotland and the Orkneys, reaching her base on 20 April. I was immediately dispatched to a prisoner of war camp at Karlsruhe, and later transferred to Freiburg, where I remained until the end of the war.

The U-62 and Captain Hashagen both survived the war; he and Commander Lewis and their families later became friends.

German naval courtesy also extended to the survivors of the destroyer HMS *Nomad*, sunk at Jutland on 31 May 1916. One of them was Able Seaman J. A. D. Byrne.

> Our fleet was steaming on a similar course to that of the enemy and was soon out of sight, there we were left bailing out our boat with our caps. We had a few wounded with us, and a few in the

carley float; we also had a few killed, and I think that we were lucky to be alive after the broadsides the enemy had put into our ship. We had been paddling about, watching hopelessly the enemy ships passing by about four miles away; there seemed to be hundreds of them, and the last but one in their line turned and steamed towards us and took us on board. They were good to us in the Navy and gave us some black bread, coffee and fish, and we were refreshed. As time went on the ship steamed up and joined the others; it was dark by now and the sea was getting very rough. The German sailors bade us sleep, but that was out of the question as we were still thinking about those that had gone down in our ship. During the night the British were chasing the Germans, and we had many scares; it was lucky for us we were in a fast ship, and managed to avoid action with the British. If the ship that we were held prisoners in had been sunk we would have gone down in it like rats in a trap, because the sentry had been ordered to keep us below till we arrived in harbour the next morning.

Despite growing evidence to the contrary, stories of German 'frightfulness' to captured Allied soldiers continued to circulate as the war went on; no one, it appeared, was exempt from brutal treatment at the hands of the Hun – in contrast, of course, to the courtesy offered to captured Germans by the British and their allies – and so when Captain R. Tennant Bruce, a medical officer with the 152nd Infantry Brigade, 51st Highland Division, was captured on 23 November 1917 during the Battle of Cambrai he faced the immediate future with some trepidation. His fears, however, were quickly allayed.

Bruce, together with a padre, the Reverend Andrew Grant, MC, had been reconnoitring the Cambrai battlefield with a view to establishing aid posts when the couple stumbled on some German positions and were captured. Bruce later recalled:

Two very young lads, with open and cheerful countenances, were placed in charge of us, given their orders, and we were marched off through the wood in a northerly direction. I don't know how the padre felt, but for my part the shock was pretty great and I felt most horribly depressed. At one moment we were free and having a walk which was enjoyable enough considering where we were and what was afoot; the next we were prisoners. . . . My

17

guard was a mere lad, I should think about nineteen, most likely a farm labourer from some quiet country spot. There had been at first unpleasant glances all around us at the fort, but once it was known it was a case of 'Arzt' and 'Pfarrer' (Doctor and Priest) these changed to good-humoured amusement.

After perfunctory questioning at Bourlon village Bruce and Grant were taken on a hair-raising truck ride through heavy British shellfire and then marched several miles to Sailly Lestrem, where

We were marched into an imposing house in a garden, probably a Brigade HQ. Inside we were again questioned, but only in a perfunctory way. Lunch was on the table and one Boche officer was loudly partaking. Another was poring over a map at the 'phone. We were not offered food, though very ready for it. An officer then buttoned on his coat and beckoned us to follow. A fine touring car awaited him and into it we all got, the officer saying to us, 'Gentleman, you are my prisoners.'

From accounts given to us by other officer inmates later on we realized how fortunate we were to be driven. Possibly the fact of our being non-combatants and not in the first bloom of youth had to do with our luck in this respect! We were taken to quite a large chateau about ten miles distant, evidently newly taken on as HQ, as the telephones were in the course of being installed. We learnt later that Cambrai had been evacuated hurriedly, fearing its capture by our troops, and this was one of the fresh HQ. Lunch was being served, and we did not know whether we hoped to be offered any or not. We were frightfully hungry, but also very dirty, and cut poor figures as British officers. I was unshaven, and both of us were wearing the oldest of breeches and tunics, much disfigured by the muck picked up during the battle. However, there was no invitation, and we remained hungry.

I had no idea what time it was, as my watch had broken down. . . . More perfunctory questioning, and we were conducted to what was possibly Corps HQ, and then to the office of the Intelligence Department. . . . Then came the real questioning, and for this we were taken separately. . . . The questions were put abruptly, not to say roughly, but there was no real impoliteness. Of course, every attempt was made to extract information, but on our denial there was no real 'frightfulness'.

. . . Two new guards now took us in charge and marched us to the Town Major's, where a chit was given us for a meal. This was afforded at what seemed to be a newly opened soldiers' club kitchen, a beautifully equipped and spotlessly clean apartment. There we ate soup, bread and sausage, and were removed later to the guardroom, a long, large wooden hut with a stove at one end, four wire beds on each side of the room, some forms, a table and half a dozen soldiers. They were decent fellows, quite ready to be amicable, and set us down by the fire and tried to talk to us . . . every now and then a soldier got up, buckled on his equipment and disappeared, while others, whose spell on guard was over, returned to the comfort and ease of the guardroom. Their politeness of manner and instinctive avoidance of offence nearly equalled that of our own men in similar circumstances.

When harsh treatment was meted out to prisoners of war – by both sides, it must be said – this usually occurred when a major offensive was in progress. It was a fact of war; when a forward position was captured it had to be consolidated as quickly as possible, which meant that prisoners had to be urged out of it and pushed back to the rear without ceremony. This was particularly apparent during the overwhelming German spring offensives of 1918, which almost succeeded in splitting the Allied armies asunder. The ensuing chaos is well illustrated in the diary of one anonymous soldier:

12 April 1918. Captured this morning at 5.0 a.m. at Le Cornet Malo. Had no chance. Completely surrounded. Jerry relieved each one of their valuables, even taking the leather gaiters of a dispatch rider. . . . Carrying wounded until 7.0 p.m. Wounded laid out in rows in paddock adjoining farm at Neuve Chapelle. Only one doctor and one Red Cross man to attend to them. Absolute chaos, bandages made of paper. Had no food since last night.

13 April. Slept in the open last night. There was a frost. Damned cold. Had some boiled potatoes this morning. First food we have had. Went round rows of wounded and picked out the dead ready for burial. Dug a hole about 9 ft wide, 14 ft long and 6 ft deep. Into this we had to place dead bodies, head towards the outer edge. Four or five rows like this, and we had to stand on dead to lay them in evenly. One of the last was an old French lady who

had been killed the day before . . . the last body to be placed in the hole was that of one of our own airmen, whose machine was brought down the day before about 100 yards away. . . . I had to search his pockets for anything that would identify him, but there was nothing. His shoulder straps had South Africa on them and one of these I cut off and gave to Jerry. When the grave was filled in the top body was only about a foot below ground level. No burial service, nothing to mark who or what they were, English, German and a civilian all together, poor devils.

After complaining about the food or the lack of it, we were given a wounded man between four and told to follow the road. We didn't know where we were going, but wherever it was it couldn't be worse than Neuve Chapelle. On the way our shells fell quite close enough and I'm afraid the wounded had a rough passage. . . . Made our way to Marquilles, where there was a prison camp. Hungry as can be. Only boiled potatoes since we were taken prisoner. We were looking forward to a meal when we arrived at this camp but we were disappointed. Eight men to a small loaf in the morning and six at night.

17 April. Still here. Hoping each day to leave for a proper camp. One of the guards gave me a herring today. Never tasted raw fish before, but then I have never been so hungry. Guard told me (in broken French) that fish was exported from England to Holland who sold it to Germany. It therefore helped to feed the German troops. If such is the case, what a farce.

21 April. Went for a bath this morning and had clothes fumigated. Mine wanted it badly. Shirt almost walking, although I have tried to keep the little devils down. Taken to a camp at Illies afterwards. Food is supposed to be better here. I hope so. I'm feeling as weak as can be. . . .

22 April. Paraded at 5.0 a.m. Interpreter asked if anyone wanted to go sick and one man unwisely said he did. The officer came and looked at him, and then gave him a punch in the face which knocked him down. . . .

30 April. We are still at this awful place. The walk to Frohmelles and back each day (for work duty, carrying bricks) is getting me down. We drop down exhausted when we return. Yesterday we saw one of our men tied to a tree when we got back and found

that he had stolen a piece of bread belonging to one of the men. Our own men had therefore tied him up as a punishment. I don't know how long he had been there, but I can imagine the feeling which prompted him to steal the bread: gnawing hunger.

The chaos attending the 1918 spring offensive is also reflected in the account of Captain G. D. J. McMurtrie of the Somerset Light Infantry, who was taken prisoner in March at Cambrai. His report reveals something else, too, which also has a bearing on the enemy's treatment of newly captured prisoners: the weary and dispirited nature of the German troops, despite their successes.

In the middle of Villers St Christophe we halted at an old English casualty clearing station, which was crowded with wounded, both German and English, with others waiting outside to be dressed. German doctors were working very hard. One, who knew a little English, seeing that I was an officer, called me to him. He was attending an English private, belonging to the Shropshire Light Infantry and the 20th Division, who was very badly wounded and dying. He died whilst I was talking to the doctor and the doctor gave me his identity discs and a letter from his mother and asked me to write and tell her how he died. . . .

It was a pitiable sight at the CCS. There were crowds of wounded, some groaning and crying out in their extreme pain, others waiting patiently to be tended, there were dead and dying everywhere, bandages and blood, stretchers and wounded. We did not wait there long and soon formed up with another batch of prisoners. . . . We began a tiring march to St Quentin and were told that we should get food and rest there. We passed one huge long line of infantry, gunners, transport and reserves of all kinds. Four things struck me on this march. One was the extraordinary absence of any enthusiasm on the part of the German troops. Here they were in the middle of a great advance, breaking through at all points, and yet no light-heartedness, none of that exhilarating high spirits, which was always to be seen and felt in the British Army. If we had made such a successful attack at this, every officer and man, be he in the front line or right in the rear, would be mad with excitement and delight, everyone would be laughing and joking and seeing the humorous side of discomfort and fatigue and danger. But here I felt that the sentiment of the

German troops was 'When is this awful show to end, I will have to go on, but I'm tired out, I'm starved and I have no interest. I only want peace and home.'

The second thing was the deplorable state the transport was in. There were poor bony horses, looking starved, with ribs sticking out, awful old waggons, which might fall to pieces at any moment without the slightest warning. There were no well-fed horses, and good GS waggons, which one always associated with the British Army. It looked like a procession of farmers with their waggons and not soldiers with the transport of a great army.

The third thing was the extraordinary mixture of young boys and old men who seemed to make up the Reserves. The front line troops were soldiers and good soldiers at that, the rest were but civilians in uniform. There was no marching discipline, no smartness, no decent uniform – just civilians in patched-up clothes, tramping along, almost bored to tears. If a man was severely wounded, he was left to die; if a man was slightly wounded but could walk, he was bandaged up and then left to make his own way to the nearest aid post and then back to Germany as best he could, sometimes walking, sometimes getting on lorries. There were no Battalion stretcher-bearers, no ambulances, no ambulance trains. . . .

We passed a great many dead and crossed the original front line from which they had driven us. All the dead, both ours and the enemy's, had been stripped of their boots and sometimes of their clothes. Germany wanted leather, Germany wanted clothes and badly.

The message was clear. By the spring of 1918 Germany no longer had the resources to meet the basic needs of her own troops, let alone provide the bare necessities of life for hundreds of thousands of prisoners. Without the help of outside agencies, POWs would have experienced starvation, disease, and death on an unprecedented scale.

Senior rank sometimes brought its own privileges on capture, but not always. Brigadier-General H. C. Rees, commanding the 158th Brigade, was taken prisoner on the Aisne on 28 May 1918; he had an interview with the Kaiser, who was inspecting his front-line troops, and was then taken by car to Marle, an army HQ, where he was very well treated.

I talked for a few minutes with an officer, who said he had been in India and asked if I wanted anything. I said I wanted some food as I hadn't had anything for about 50 hours, so he said 'we won't let you starve' and sent me off to the officers' club, where they knocked up the club steward and gave me bacon and eggs and beer. I was given a very comfortable room for the night, breakfast next morning, and at 1 p.m. was taken again to lunch at the club by two officers, who spoke English. The treatment I received with this HQ was everything which would be wished.

On 30 May Rees was taken to the town of Hirson, and there the privileged treatment ended.

I was placed in the fort and put in a very small whitewashed cell. I was not allowed out of this cell on any pretext, except that I was allowed on the ramparts for half an hour one day, so timed that I could watch some 6,000 prisoners march past the fort. There was nobody that could speak English and I could only make any requests through a French boy, who acted as my orderly and swept out the cell. Conditions in this fort were really diabolical. The window of my cell, which overlooked the central courtyard, was set at an angle which enabled me to see a line of cell windows. These cells contained French and Belgian political offenders, who were confined by whole families and who were horribly starved and desperate looking.

The food given me was ½ pint of acorn coffee and a lump of black bread at 8 a.m. Half a canteen full of vegetable soup at midday. The rest could be eaten at supper and that was all. On two days, I had a twist of paper with either jam or potted meat in it. On this ration, one starves.

Corporal Arthur Speight of the 7th Durham Light Infantry, captured on the Aisne on 26 May 1918, experienced rough treatment. The Germans rifled the prisoners' pockets, and then

We were kicked, thumped, jabbed in the ribs with rifle butts and generally made to feel that we were, to say the least, superfluous. We were forcibly propelled on to the road and made to carry machine guns forward towards the bridge. In a short while we were hustled back to the cutting where other fellows had also been collected. With this lot we were marched up towards our former home passing large parties of Germans coming down the hill.

In the rear area, Speight and the others were set to work burying British dead who had lain out in the open for about a fortnight. After that they were compelled to load shells on to ammunition trucks at Pontavert, then taken back to rudimentary billets at Ramecourt.

The conditions now were even worse than before . . . the latrine accommodation consisted merely of a hole in the ground, no disinfectant whatever being provided and everything being most offensive. Washing accommodation was conspicuous by its complete absence. The place had been taken over by a company of Landwehr . . . and a more spiteful set of old devils could not have been found anywhere. Their title was Bewachungs-Kompagnie II 33. Their behaviour was atrocious.

In contrast to the behaviour of these reserve troops, Speight tells how kindness was shown by front-line soldiers. The British prisoners were repairing a railway line near Amifontaine.

The recognized loads for carrying were one sleeper per man, ten men to a rail, and in our half-starved state these loads were fearful. Quite a number of men ruptured themselves but Fritz didn't seem to worry about that. . . . Here the trains were running up to the line and returning therefrom and we were bombarded by soldiers from the trenches with chunks of bread and cigarettes, much in the same way that our fellows going on leave used to take pot shots at Jerry with biscuits, bully beef and tins of jam. We always found that those Germans who were coming from the trenches were fairly decent to us, very different from the guardian angels who were usually in attendance on us.

One guard, in his generosity, allowed the prisoners to collect snails from the hedgerows and cook them.

Speight and his fellow prisoners were kept at work on the railways in the rear area as the summer wore on. They were forced labourers; the German offensive of 1918 had come to a halt and everything now depended on maintaining a flow of men and supplies to the front. Treatment here was far worse than that experienced in most prison camps in Germany, as Speight records. This was especially true to the rations, which were appalling.

We began our day's work by being walked on and walloped with sticks while it was still dark. Then we were shoved into lines of

24

four men and issued with a drink of coffee made from burnt barley. A piece of bread was the day's ration but as most of the fellows were nearly mad for food the first one got the most – if he was strong enough to keep it! Our work would carry on until about five in the afternoon. . . . On arriving at the lager we were issued with another meal. This meal consisted of stewed something. At first this was sometimes macaroni with a very little meat mixed with it. By about June it had become dried vegetables. This mess of pottage consisted of turnip skins dried almost to resemble chips of wood, chopped up like sawdust and mixed with boiling water. . . .

The worst thing in so-called eatables arrived about August. This was spinach pickled in tubs of sea water and just boiled . . . the meat ration was practically a myth but now and again we got some horses' lights . . . it was a case of shut your eyes and hope for the best. Twice we were favoured with a ration of meat which one of our guards told me was seal. It was dark red in colour and had a strong taste and of course may have been anything. These evening meals were usually well salted so our nights were usually made miserable by extreme thirst which could not be allayed.

Inevitably, the prisoners suffered a severe outbreak of dysentery and began to die. Speight recalled that

It was a common sight to see about six men pulling a cart through the village with about twenty dead men piled on it ready for burial, the whole being followed by a cloud of flies. . . . This sort of thing went on for some time and I often used to think of the tales I had read of Englishmen standing out in time of trouble as patterns of calm dignity. Compared with the story-book Englishman I am afraid our chaps fell a terribly long way short of the required standard but you must always bear in mind that for the most part they were lads of 19 years of age. . . . One incident stands out in my mind which should give some idea as to the state some of these men had come to. The ration of bread had evidently been issued from old stock and was quite unfit to eat, being bright green in colour. Corporal Costello took the whole ration, sorted out what might be eatable, and to make sure of none of the bad bread finding its way to the sick men, he threw it into the open latrine. Two wrecks of humanity crawled to the latrine on hands and knees and plunged their arms into the filth to recover the bread. Costello yelled at them that the stuff would kill them, but still they were intent on getting it, whereupon Costello ran forward and flung them bodily from the hole. He then turned away and said: 'Well, I don't know, the poor —s will die anyway.'

Yet it was not all like this. Another British prisoner, Private Reginald T. Bellamy, captured at Cambrai on 28 March 1918, has little to say by way of complaint in his diary of subsequent events. Bellamy was put to work on the roads, loading wagons, and a variety of other tasks. The food at first was not very good, but by June it had improved substantially. 'Had a very good dinner on 5th. Thick meaty stew. Billet is also far better.' And, in July:

14. A very good day for rations: ¼ loaf for breakfast and tea and ½ herring for breakfast. Fish, sour cabbage and meal for dinner (bought some extra) and also got 'buckshee'. Finished with coffee and cigarette. Church service tonight. . . .

15. Very good barley and meal dinner with plenty of meat. . . .

17. An easy day. ¼ loaf and cheese for breakfast and good clear soup and fruit dinner. . . .

26. Very good day for rations. Splendid thick dinner of barley meal and meat and I got nearly another issue as it was my 'buckshee' day. For tea an issue of cucumber from the French and an extra supper of meal and fresh vegetable (French).

Bellamy and his fellow prisoners seem to have enjoyed plenty of reading material, too. They were fortunate in that most of their work was carried out in the St Amand-les-Eaux area, a quiet backwater relatively untouched by the war, where the local French citizens were continuing with business more or less as usual; although food was in short supply locally, the French willingly parted with what they had. Speight, on the other hand, was in an area not far from Reims; here, the German spring offensive had brought their forces to within forty miles of Paris, and the pressure was on to regain the momentum. Prisoner comforts here were very much a secondary consideration, if indeed they were considered at all. As always, the treatment depended very much on where, when, and by whom men were captured.

Chapter 3

INSIDE THE CAMPS, 1914–17

It was to the infamous camp at Sennelager, in Westphalia, that many of the British Expeditionary Force troops taken prisoner in the great retreat of 1914 were taken. Sennelager was a large military training centre where, in the words of the anonymous NCO of the 1st Hampshires:

> We came in for rather bad treatment and had our share of kicks and jeers at the hands of the soldiery there. They thought it was particularly reprehensible that we should have *volunteered* to fight for our country!
>
> I was at once removed to the hospital hut and put into bed. My wounds were dressed by one of our own RAMC men, and after three days in bed I was turned out of hospital and put on the ground in the open air to make room for someone else to take my bed. I was out in the open day and night, and after a few days about 200 English and French wounded soldiers arrived and suffered the same treatment. We were exposed to the sun, rain, cold, flies and kicks! After five days in the open air I was placed in hospital again as my wounds were getting gangrenous through neglect. After about three weeks I was able to get about with the aid of a stick and was able to wash myself. I was then sent up to the camp again to the other prisoners but had to attend hospital each day, for six weeks.
>
> At that time [October 1914] there were about 4,000 English prisoners in the Sennelager camp, including a Church of England Padre, Major Hales, six MOs, and all the French prisoners who were taken at Maubeuge – about 40,000 of them. At the end of my six weeks attendance at the hospital, I asked the German MO to give me a paper stating that I was not fit for work. He did this,

but the certificate was of little use, for the next morning I was ordered out on fatigue at 4.30 a.m. to carry wood up to the camp. This I found was too much for me as I was still very weak. On my return to camp Sgt Jeffery told me I was wanted at the Commandant's office at 3 p.m., and then I discovered I had been recommended to be sent to another camp. The change appealed to me as I was convinced that there could not be a worse camp in Germany. We were all verminous and we could not keep clean, try how we would. My next camp was Gütersloh, which on arrival I found was to be a camp for all the Allied officers.

Another soldier who endured the misery of Sennelager was Corporal John Brady of the King's Own Yorkshire Light Infantry, captured at Le Cateau on 26 August 1914. Later in the war, when he was in Holland awaiting repatriation because of desperate ill health occasioned by the treatment he had received during his captivity, he wrote of his experiences in a letter to his wife and children, a document all the more touching for its rough, semi-literate honesty. On arrival at Sennelager he and his fellow captives were issued with a little bread. Then, after a sleepless night without blankets:

Next morning we received bread and coffee we had a bath and our hair cut like a convict at Dinner time we received half a pint of soup we was just going like skeletons too weak to walk we had seven day on the sand without any blankets or straw all we could hear was stand up English swines then they erected us a tent and gave us a blanket each and some straw our Daily food Morning bread and sausage Midday soup consisting of water we was just about starving I took very ill I thought my time had come and then the lice started. Millions of them Daily I was three months and never had a wash with soap I only had one shirt never was washed for three months all that time we had to go out to work if we were sick and the Doctor said work you got kicked out from August till January without a change of a shirt or draws then we got wooden huts but no beds.

In December 1914 Brady received two Red Cross parcels, their enjoyment marred by illness. Christmas dinner, provided by the Germans, was

potato and a bit of carrot floating in water. Men was going mad with cold and hunger in January . . . things went on just the same till I was sent away with twenty-three others to work in a stone quarry and we had to work very hard. Our parcels delayed several weeks it was torture to have to work on the food received from Germans not fit for a pig but we could not write home and state the situation as our letters would be burnt and we would be punished so we had to write and say we was in good health at the time we was dying of starvation.

By July 1915 Brady and the others in his work party decided they had had enough. Brady told the German corporal in charge that conditions were too bad to work and that the men were going on strike.

I thought he was going mad . . . you must get your men to work you swine out came his revolver and call for the sentrys to fix bayonets . . . we still refused so he cooled down . . . then we had a bit of a rough time till 12 am when a Captain and Corporal and fifteen Germans came to the place the very first thing I saw the sentrys charging Magazines and fixing bayonets then I thought our time had come then we were fell in on parade.

Brady and the others were put in prison. The Yorkshireman was held to be the instigator of the 'mutiny' and told that he was to be placed on trial, with a strong possibility that he would be shot. In the event, however, the Germans conducted the proceedings with scrupulous fairness.

An officer came from Berlin and told me he was our solicitor so I told him all I knew and what he did he said he would do his very best for us but we stood on a charge of mutiny and rebellion I don't mind telling you I did not sleep that night the next morning at 10 am we were in court the case lasted four hours. Our solicitor spoke very well for us so we were found guilty of Mutiny and sentenced to six months with hard labour, we were all smiles after that some said they could do that on their head. Two days later we were sent to a civil prison not too bad plenty of work wood sawing but we were not allowed any parcels were stayed only a month and went to Coln . . . we had a very rough time out of our party one died and another were taken to hospital I did not see him any more.

Brady finished his sentence in February 1916 in a very weakened condition and was sent back to Sennelager. After two weeks he was put to work sweeping the streets of Paderborn, a task accompanied by frequent beatings. A refusal to work in a mine brought him another fourteen days in the cells, then he was transferred to Minden, 'another terrible camp . . . two months before I received another parcel so I had to live like a pig again, pigs in England receive better food'.

Brady and a fellow prisoner were ordered to work in a nearby wire factory, alongside sixty Frenchmen, but the place produced barbed wire of the kind used at the front, so they refused, whereupon

> the Corporal lost his temper and struck us with his bayonet and kicked us around the room then I said to my pal stick it Harry we will get over it so at 4 pm we were marched to prison I thought my pal were going to break down his first time in prison we stayed seven days and returned back to that place [the wire factory].

Once again Brady and his colleague refused to participate in what was clearly war work, and so the German corporal

> told us we would have to stand to attention from 5 am to 9 pm on a slice of bread daily till we would work. We stuck it eight days and were sent to another place where the officer asked us if we would work on the land. We told him yes.

The new job, Brady records, involved not much work and plenty of food, but it lasted only a month before they were again transferred to another place of work to which Brady

> took a dislike on first arriving. . . . I were asked what trade I were I told the officer blacksmith . . . my pal had to go in the pit so I told him to refuse but he was broken hearted and went to work so I went to have a look at this shop I thought it was not too bad I would give it a trial it were nothing concerning the war.

He was told that this was his last chance; either he worked or he would be killed. He was now in prison camp at Münster, which he states contained 1,400 Russians, 700 Frenchmen, and two Englishmen. Brady was soon in trouble for striking a German civilian worker; 'when I returned to camp I were struck by several sentrys and put into cells black and blue'. He stayed there for fourteen days on bread and water.

When my time were up I once more refused to go out to work well I were just about killed and kicked into a cell 28 days before I seed anyone I suffered very much in the 28 days . . . then I started planning to escape.

The appalling nature of prison camp conditions during 1914–15 is reflected, too, in the diary of Corporal C. E. Green of the Scots Guards, captured in October 1914, who, after a long rail journey, arrived at Schneidemühl, near Posen in Silesia, on 2 November 1914.

Marching about three kilometers, we sighted the camp, then in course of erection. It was a bitter cold morning . . . we were clothed only in khaki, our (great)coats having been taken away. . . . For two or three hours we were kept there. Then they started, fifty men at a time, to inoculate us. This over, we were issued with blankets, spoons, and basins, marched to the cookhouse, and given pig meal and potatoes. Although hungry, very few of us ate it. . . .

3.11.14. This morning before dawn we were down waiting for breakfast, consisting of bread and coffee. In the ensuing rush and scramble with the Russians, Pte. Bowlam of the Coldstreams was struck by a sentry. The Englishman, after holding on to his bayonet, escaped, but was afterwards caught, and thrashed by order of the officer in command. He subsequently died over this affair, his brain having been hurt. A Court of Enquiry was held, and a letter, practically an apology, was written by the officer concerned.

The prisoners at Schneidemühl were accommodated in barracks with sixty men to a room. The first parcels arrived in December, together with letters from home. Also in December typhus broke out, and within three months every English prisoner except eleven had been hospitalized with the fever. The death toll among the Russians averaged thirty a day; eleven thousand died in eight months. Twenty Britons also died, although – as Green points out – this was a larger percentage than the Russians, many thousands of whom were in the camp. The sufferings of the men were not alleviated by an order that compelled them to take two hours of exercise each day, in frost, rain, and snow, and often without trousers when these were being fumigated.

31

There was no escape from the misery of camps such as Schneidemühl; the problems of reaching neutral territory from such places were virtually insurmountable. From camps in western and southern Germany, however, the prospect of escape was brighter, although in 1915 little or no escape organization existed and attempts were usually doomed to failure, often because would-be escapers could not rely on the discretion of fellow prisoners. The anonymous NCO of the 1st Hampshires recalled that

The thought of escape had often come to me before, but whilst at Gütersloh definite plans for getting away took shape. I took a fellow prisoner, one Bishop of the RFA, into my confidence. Our scheme was to hide in the dust cart which collected the refuse from the camp at 2 p.m. each day and took it outside the wire to some refuse dump. Bishop and I tossed up as to who should go first. I won. I managed to get into the wagon at about 12.30, when all the other prisoners and the guard were having their dinner, and covered myself up with all the filth and dirt of the camp. At 2 p.m. I heard a Russian Pole tell the German civilian who acted as dustman that an Englishman was missing from working parade . . . the wagon was searched and I was discovered in it.

One camp where the prisoners remained a thorn in their captors' flesh was at Ingolstadt in Bavaria. It was designated Fort 9, and in the summer of 1916 the Germans concentrated 150 Allied officers with the blackest characters there, in much the same way that they were to turn Colditz Castle into a secure prison for habitual offenders in a later war. It was a grave error on their part, and doubly so since Ingolstadt was within striking distance of the Swiss frontier. One officer who spent some time there was Major A. J. Evans of the Royal Flying Corps, who was shot down behind the German lines on 16 July 1916. He later recalled:

When I arrived at Fort 9, Ingolstadt, seventy-five per cent of the prisoners were scheming and working continually to escape again. Escaping, and how it should be done, was the most frequent subject of conversation. In fact, the camp was nothing less than an escaping club. We pooled our knowledge and each man was ready to help anyone who wished to escape, quite regardless of his own risk or the punishment he might bring upon himself. No-one cared twopence for courts martial, and nearly everyone in the fort had done considerable spells of solitary confinement. . . . There were some of the most ingenious people in Fort 9 that I've ever met, particularly among the French, and attempts to escape took place at least once a week.

The winter of 1916 was a hard one, and the moat froze over, and although the Germans went round in a boat every day and tried to keep the ice broken, they eventually had to give it up. It was difficult to know whether the ice would bear or not, but I tested it as well as I could by throwing stones on to it, and decided one morning that I would risk it and make a dash across the moat that evening. A man named Wilkin, and Kicq, a little Belgian officer who had accompanied me on my previous attempt to escape, agreed to come with me.

Our plan was to start when the 'Appell' or roll-call bell went at 5 p.m., for it got dark soon afterwards, and I trusted that this would cover our flight. We had to run down a steep bank on to the ice, about forty yards across the ice, and then another two hundred yards or so before we could put a cottage between ourselves and the sentries. There was sure to be some shooting, but we reckoned the men's hands would be very cold, for they would already have been two hours at their posts. Moreover, they were only armed with old French rifles, which they handled badly.

We arranged with some of the other officers to create a diversion when the roll-call went by yelling and throwing stones on to the ice to distract the attention of the two nearest sentries. Our main anxiety was: would the ice bear? I felt confident it would. Wilkin said he was awfully frightened, but would go on with it. Kicq said that if I was confident, so was he. It would be extremely unpleasant if the ice broke, for we would be wearing a lot of very heavy clothes. Still, anyone who thinks too much of what may happen will never escape from prison. We filled our rucksacks with rations for a ten days' march and enough solidified alcohol for at least one hot drink a day. We then concealed them and our coats at the jumping-off place.

A few minutes before the bell went we were all three dressed and in our places. It was a bad few minutes. At last it rang, and almost immediately I heard laughter and shouting and the sound of stones falling on the ice. We jumped up and bolted over the path and down the slope. I was slightly ahead of the others, and when I got to the moat I gave a little jump on to the ice, thinking that if it was going to break at all it would break at the edge instead of in the middle. It didn't break, and I shuffled across at good speed. When I was about halfway over I heard furious yells of 'Halt!' behind me, followed by a fair amount of shooting; but I was soon up the bank on the far side and through a few scattered trees. Then I looked back.

The others were only just clambering up the bank from the moat, and were a good hundred yards behind me. It turned out that, instead of taking a little jump on the ice as I had done, they'd stepped carefully on to the edge, which had broken under their weight, and they had fallen flat on their faces. Wilkin had somehow got upside down, his heavy rucksack falling over his head, so that he couldn't move, but Kicq had freed himself and pulled Wilkin out.

The covering parties had done their job well. They'd managed to divert the attention of the most formidable sentry until I was well on the ice. He had then noticed me, yelled 'Halt!' loaded his rifle as fast as possible, dropped on one knee, fired and missed. Cold fingers, abuse and some stones hurled at him by the party on the ramparts above had not helped to steady his aim. After one or two shots his rifle jammed. Yells and cheers from the spectators. He tore at the bolt, cursing and swearing, and then put up his rifle at the crowd of jeering prisoners above him, but they could see that the bolt hadn't gone home, and only yelled louder.

Meanwhile I'd nearly reached the cottage when I saw a large, four-horse wagon on the main road on my right with a number of civilians by it. They were only about 150 yards away, and they started after us, led by a strong, healthy-looking fellow with a cart whip. The going through the snow was heavy, especially with the weight we were carrying; so the carter quickly overtook me and slashed me across the shoulders with his whip. I turned and rushed at him, but he jumped out of my reach. His companions then arrived, and I saw, too, some armed soldiers coming on bicycles along the road from the fort.

The game was up, and the next thing to do was to avoid being shot in the excitement of recapture. So I beckoned the smallest man and said in German: 'Come here and I'll give myself up to you.' The chap with the whip immediately came forward. 'No, not to you,' I said; 'you hit me with that whip.' The little fellow was very pleased, for there was a hundred marks reward for the capture of an officer, so he hung on to my coat-tails as we started back to the fort. I tore up my map and dropped it into a stream as we went.

The scene in the Commandant's office was quite amusing. We were stripped and searched. I had nothing more to hide, but both Kicq and Wilkin had compasses, which they smuggled through with great skill. Kicq's was hidden in the lining of his coat, and Wilkin had his in his handkerchief, which he pulled out of his pocket and waved to show that there was nothing in it. All our foodstuffs and clothes were returned to us, except my tin of solidified alcohol. I protested, but in vain. I was given a receipt for it and told I could have it back at the end of the war. As we left the office I saw it standing almost within my reach, and nearly managed to pocket it as I went out. However, I found a friend of mine – a French officer – outside and explained to him the position of the tin, and suggested that he should go in with a few pals and steal it back for me under cover of a row.

This was the kind of joke that the Frenchmen loved, and they were past-masters at it. They were always rushing off to the Commandant's office with frivolous complaints about one thing and another, just for a rag, which never failed to reduce the Commandant and his officers to a state of dithering rage. Within ten minutes I had my solid alcohol back all right, and kept my receipt for it as well.

At about this time an officer named Medlicott and I learnt that some Frenchmen were trying to escape across the frozen moat by cutting a window-bar in the latrines which overlooked it. The Germans, however, smelt a rat, but though they inspected the bars carefully they couldn't find the cuts, which had been artfully sealed up with a mixture of flour and ashes. Then the Feldwebel went round and shook each bar violently in turn until the fourth one came off in his hands and he fell down flat on his back. They then wired up the hole, but Medlicott and I saw a chance of cutting the wire and making another bolt for it about a week later, and we took it. We were only at large, however, for about two hours. The snow on the ground gave our tracks away; we were pursued, surrounded, and eventually had to surrender again. This time we had a somewhat hostile reception when we got back to the fort.

They searched us and took away my tin of solidified alcohol again. They recognized it. 'I know how you stole this back,' said the senior clerk as he gave me another receipt for it, 'but you shan't have it any more.' We both laughed over it. I laughed last, however, as I stole it back again in about a week's time, and kept my two receipts for it as well.

It may seem extraordinary that we were not punished severely for these attempts to escape, but there were no convenient cells in which to punish us. All the cells at Fort 9 were always full, and there was a long waiting list besides.

There was hardly any uniformity in the standard of conditions, and for that matter the treatment meted out to the inmates, in the various German POW camps in 1916. This is well illustrated in Captain Champion's account; after his spell in the 'Black Hole of Cologne' the RFC officer was transferred to the camp at Mainz early in March 1916.

We arrived at Mainz before dawn, and were taken to a canteen where we had our first taste of synthetic coffee. As soon as it was light our warrant-officer took us out and whilst going through the station the women rushed at us calling us 'Schweinhunds' and other things. The young private tried to keep them off, but could not keep their tongues quiet or stop them expectorating on us. . . . We were put in a large room on the ground floor overlooking a quadrangle. We saw our late escort being 'strafed' by an officer for something or other; this amused us considerably. . . .

At 8.30 the square started to fill with Russian, French, Belgian and British officers. They formed up in companies and counted. There were about 600 in all. The British seemed to be in a bad way judging by the state of their uniforms. This was owing to the fact that they were mostly men taken at Le Cateau in 1914 and had received very little in the way of kit for eighteen months. The French consisted of prisoners taken at Maubeuge in 1914, and the more recent ones from Verdun. The commander of Maubeuge was also there, and it was rumoured that he would be shot on his return. The Huns gave him more liberty and better treatment than the ordinary prisoner.

About midday we were taken before a little Jew Intelligence Officer, who questioned us and seemed very keen to know if we intended bombing Mainz. I assured him that we had that in mind, and he seemed quite upset. Afterwards we learnt that he was a standing joke and everyone pulled his 'intelligent' leg. Herbie Ward once told him of some wonderful new machines we had, one with two propellers, one in front and one behind, the advantage of this being that the machine could fly backwards if necessary to mislead 'Archie', or hover over a spot when both propellers were in motion; by this means very accurate bombing could be accomplished.

After a meal at midday we were taken into a room where we were ordered to strip and allowed a bath. We were given back our flying coats, pants, vests and boots and set at liberty pending the return of our clothes after disinfection had been carried out. We were at once surrounded by British officers who wanted to know all the news. Amongst the prisoners were Gower of the Musters . . . Halls, born in the Cape, and Pelham-Burn who was put in cells, as were all men with hyphenated names, as a reprisal for our action in putting a captured submarine crew in cells. Grey was put in cells because they considered he must be a relation of Sir Edward Grey [the British Foreign Secretary].

We were given tea and supper by Pelham-Burn and others. We were given bunks in a room with about fifteen others, some French. The bunks were in tiers with hard boards and straw mattresses, and I slept very well.

The fellows taken at Le Cateau and about that time had some awful tales to tell of cruelty and ill-treatment. This is a subject which now seems to be forgotten and made light of, partly owing to the Leipzig Trials fiasco and present British politics. [The Leipzig War Crimes Trials were held by the German supreme court in 1921.] In spite of the trials and hardships endured by these men, their spirit was unbroken (with the exception of one old Colonel who I really think was insane due entirely to the treatment received at the hands of the Hun).

After a very short stay in Mainz Champion and his observer, Lt Newbold, were moved to Vohrenbach in the Black Forest. They knew nothing about it except that it was a new camp and that it had definite escape possibilities, being closer to the Swiss frontier. On arrival they found that it consisted of a recently completed school, a large two-storey building with a very large attic. It was surrounded by an eight-foot-high double barbed wire fence, with a single gate. The grounds were very small, not much more than an acre in all.

There were about eighty Frenchmen and four Russians already in occupation. Our party consisted of Newbold, Binny and myself, and sixteen Frenchmen. The whole country was covered in about two foot of snow; we were on the outskirts of a small village and surrounded by hills covered with pine forests. It was beautiful and the weather ideal.

The food was good compared with Mainz where, as an example, soup was made from dirty plates. This is no exaggeration. We were given a roll of black bread and eight inches long and two inches in diameter, which was supposed to last us two days. I could never manage that.

At eight o'clock we were given coffee, at midday some meat sometimes, usually macaroni and turnips, in the evening coffee again and more macaroni or potato salad. Italy at this time was not at war with Germany, and the Germans got all the macaroni they wanted. There was a canteen where one could buy or order anything one wanted except eatables. Drinkables were dirt cheap, and the Hun made no objection to anyone drinking more than was good for him. In fact I think they encouraged it. This was the cause of a considerable amount of ill-health, and many young fellows are ruined today on account of this. We received parcels from England, and practically lived on the tinned food sent. The French got very little from home and the Russians nil. The poor Russians got very little pay and could not afford to drink wine, and so I regret used methylated spirits as a substitute. . . .

We had an excellent Mess, the Huns allowed us to use spirit stoves, and we only had the midday meal at the Huns' expense. Most of the fellows had been prisoners for some time and got parcels regularly. We used to take it in turns to cook the breakfast, which consisted of oatmeal or Quaker Oats and milk and sugar, and a rasher of bacon. The suppers were much more elaborate. On my birthday my diary gives the following menu: kidney soup, poulet roti, vegetables, asparagus, trifle (our recipe), chocolates and liqueur brandy. An excellent meal, especially considering that everything was tinned.

The commandant at Vohrenbach was an easygoing general, a veteran of the Franco-Prussian War, who had been brought out of retirement. He had an English wife who originally came from Cheltenham, and gave his British prisoners an enormous amount of leeway. Apart from a wide range of in-camp amusements such as hockey and gymnastics, prisoners were allowed to take walks outside the camp provided they gave their parole that they would not try to escape. The parole was a little superfluous, as the walkers were always accompanied by an officer and an armed guard; for this reason most of the English officers refused to take advantage of the offer. The guards themselves, however, were not on the look-out for trouble; they were old men of the Landsturm, the German territorial reserve, and were always very respectful to the inmates, although they were not allowed to speak to them. In all, it was hardly surprising that when Vohrenbach was visited by neutral observers – Swiss or Spanish – there were no complaints. The same could not be said of Mainz, where complaints were constantly laid against Mecklenburg, the commandant; yet, despite promises, no action was taken against him at the post-war Leipzig Trials.

The relatively leisurely and – as far as possible under the circumstances – civilized way of life in Vohrenbach contrasted sharply with the conditions in Silesia, where other ranks were set to work in coal- and salt-mines. Late in 1915 Corporal C. E. Green of the Scots Guards was transferred from the POW camp at Schneidemühl, near Posen (later Poznań), to Bursigwerk in Oberschlesien where, accommodated in a rudimentary hostel with many other forced labourers, he was to begin a daily routine of working in the nearby Preussengrube coal-mine. The conditions underground were appalling, and it was not long before some of the weaker POWs succumbed and were taken, worn out, to hospital, some to die there. Others devised various schemes to feign illness; a favourite was to swallow half a pound of twist tobacco.

The prisoners, who were mostly guarded by Poles, shared the mining work with German and Polish civilians. On 22 March 1916, Green recalled:

> We were very lucky this day, finishing work at 2 p.m. The other shift had only been working two and a half hours when a terrible explosion occurred in the Packhammer district. I had been working in the same place for a fortnight. Fourteen Germans and eight Russians lost their lives. All available men with safety

lamps were set to work finding bodies. Three shifts all working hard at it. . . . 28 March. Six bodies buried had been found two days previously. In a horrible state. . . . 30 March. Three Germans found, one completely cut in two. . . . 3 April. The day shift found the last body, a Russian.

On 30 April a new guard suddenly arrived at the mine, composed of Saxons and Prussians. This was because the Germans had learned that the Polish miners were about to go on strike, and feared that the Polish guards might support them. On the following day the shift of which Cpl Green was a member demanded ten marks a shift, with an extra half a mark and half a pound of bacon for a ten-hour shift. The strike was short-lived and the men went back to work after a week, having secured no advantage.

The normal treatment for anyone reporting sick, Green records, was 'Aspirin und Arbeit' – aspirin and work. Only food parcels kept the POWs going, as the issue ration was 'not fit for a pig sty – never mind human consumption'. Green's diary records that in July 1916 a number of the German guards departed for the front and were replaced by others who 'looked as though they had seen much service'. He also notes that, in August, six more Englishmen arrived to begin work at the Carsten Central Mine; they had been sentenced to work there for twelve months, apparently as punishment for refusing to join an Irish Brigade which the Germans were attempting to form at Lemberg. Easter 1916 had witnessed the abortive uprising in Dublin; the Germans had taken this, quite erroneously, as a sign that there was considerable anti-English feeling among the Irish regiments in the British Army, and had gone to some lengths to try and recruit Irish 'volunteers' from the prison camps. It may have been the case that some Irishmen disliked the English, but they disliked the Germans even more, as was soon apparent from the Irish Brigade's recruiting figures.

Apart from the danger underground and the appalling rations, the main feature of life at the Preussengrube mine was one of crippling boredom. It was alleviated to some extent by an issue of newspapers; most were German propaganda organs but they were devoured eagerly, and through them the prisoners learned of such major events as the death of Lord Kitchener and the Battle of Jutland. Green tells how the prisoners refused to believe the German account of the losses sustained by both sides at Jutland; in fact they were quite true.

One man who could testify to that was Able Seaman James Byrne, captured when the destroyer HMS *Nomad* was sunk on 31 May and put ashore at Wilhelmshaven.

On June 1st our captivity really began. We were taken ashore and marched through the streets. I had one boot on and one off – I felt awful. The German population of Wilhelmshaven put their hands across their throats at us, meaning they would cut our throats, and called us swines. . . . We were eventually handed over to the military and detailed for our destinations. All of us except the wounded went to Dülmen (Westphalia), where we saw other POWs who told us what to expect. From Dülmen we went to Brandenburg, where we were inoculated four times in the chest for different diseases, and had a week off to get over it. We were overcrowded and the food was mostly potato soup, parsnips and horse meat.

Volunteers were called for to go out and work on the farm. As life in the camp was very hard most of us volunteered, as we were promised good food. Fifteen of us went to one farm and fifteen to another, or so they thought. When they got there they found it was a factory making munitions, so they all packed in. The result was starvation until they began work again; that went on for two days, then they were given other work.

Those of us working on the real farm were ordered up at about 5 a.m. and given watery porridge before we set out at 5.30. On arrival at a large potato field I was asked if I understood horses; I happen to like horses very much and so I replied that I did, whereupon they gave me a plough and three horses. I was very nervous because I didn't know the first thing about the animals. I was told how to make them go, and how to make them stop. On completing my day's work I rode the animals back to the stables. I was on the back of the middle one when all of a sudden the harness slipped round, and before I realised it I was hanging on grimly beneath the horse's body. Luckily a POW stopped the horse and I was put off; so much for that.

Back we went to our 'digs', which was a loft over a cow and sheep shed. Our beds were just straw and a blanket and we had a lot of company during the night in the form of fleas, beetles and mice. Despite these, and the continual noise from the animals below, we were so tired and hungry that we just gave in to sleep.

We were getting threepence a day and the boss had promised

us a penny rise in a couple of days. But the days passed and no
rise appeared, so we packed in and went on strike, bolting the
door of our loft. There were only two old sentries in charge and
we sat back to await events, thinking it would be easy. We didn't
have to wait long – less than twenty-four hours in fact – for early
the next morning six large Prussians came and knocked the door
down, rushing into the room with fixed bayonets and swearing
and shouting at us as loud as they could. It was no good resisting,
so we went quietly and they sent us down the steps at the double.

About a month after this the fifteen of us went back to the main
camp at Brandenburg; we were there for a week and then got
detailed for another job. This was in a factory and we were given
to understand that it had nothing to do with war work, which for
once proved to be true. We were mixed with Russian and French
POWs. We were there for a month, and during that time two
Russians were shot. As far as I could see the Russians had no-one
to look after their welfare in Germany and the Jerries took
advantage of this, bullying them all the more. It was agonising to
see the way they were treated – worse than dogs. Most of them
used to offer prayers each night. . . . Half the Russians couldn't
write their own names, most of them being large strong peasants;
they told me they had to wait in their trenches for their comrades
to be killed or wounded before they could have a rifle or machine-
gun.

The influx of Allied prisoners of war into the German camps
peaked sharply as a result of the summer offensives of 1916, and
appears to have caused some resentment among some of the longer-
serving inmates, who by this time had established their own order of
things. This was apparent to Private R. Preston of the 8th Battalion
KRRC, who, after recovering from wounds received on the Somme
in July, was moved to Langensalza in Thuringia.

There were double rows of barbed wire all over and large wooden
pylons with machine guns built at strategic positions. There were
also separate huts for English, French and Russian prisoners. We
were taken to the English post and found that we were under the
command of English guardsmen who had been captured earlier
on and were quite at home to our way of thinking. One of the men
came to speak to me and asked if I was a guardsman as I was now
about six feet tall but still rather skinny. I told him that I was a

42

Kitchener's Army man and thought he was going to reply by spitting on the floor like that German officer did [a reference to an earlier incident]. So I told him where to go as that was all I could do, because I hadn't really regained much strength yet.

Many arguments broke out as to whose bunk was whose and the guardsmen seemed to have access to food whether it was Red Cross issued or not – but we didn't get any. We were obviously not wanted here. The Russians were given cooking duties but the tanks filled with soup were filthy. There was mud in the potatoes and vegetables whilst a type of fish was just chopped in half. If it had been cleaned properly it would have been edible but I tried to clean it without any great success, so I was there for three days with practically nothing to eat.

One day the spokesman for the Guards called us together and told us that a parade would be held by the German authorities the following morning in order to place us in working parties. We were notified that if any of us volunteered for any job, our names and regiments would be recorded and when the war was over we would receive our punishment at home. On assembly, there were about fifty soldiers present and on the first call of volunteers – for farm workers – one man stepped forward. The same thing happened on the next two calls. I thought they must be either old members of the camp or they were cronies of the Guards who had been reminded of the easy jobs. The rest of us just stood waiting.

The officer in charge then divided us into three sections. Some were for coaling on railway sidings, some were for sugar beet factories and the last twenty-six of us were to be sent to the salt mines – a dreaded place we had heard, especially from reading history books. We were marched to a narrow gauge railway siding and sent through the countryside to Bad Rastenburg, which used to be a watering place and a health resort before the sinking of the mine for precious salt. Confronting us was a large army hut with a central passage; it was divided into separate rooms and had been occupied by Russian prisoners and a few Frenchmen. Four Russians were still confined to their rooms. We were soon told that there was no food as the kitchen staff had gone home for the day. . . .

Our rooms were arranged to hold twelve men in each – there were six in my room and eight in the next. Double-tiered beds were fitted in each room away from the door and window, leaving sufficient room for a small table in the middle and for us all to sit on the lower beds. My bunk was on top with the foot of the bed near to the window, which was barred and fixed open about two inches for a little fresh air. The first morning we were given thick bean soup, but the cooks sometimes varied it by giving us cabbage soup with carraway seed or soured potato soup. There was no meat whatsoever. We were offered tinned blood between two slices of black bread for a midday snack which we took down the mine. Ersatz coffee was available in an enamel container in the passage but we had to be careful drinking it, for we found that the burnt malt coffee gave us heartburn and the burnt acorn coffee upset our bowels.

Our first morning to work . . . could have been frightening for some of the lads, but I was used to such things, having been familiar with the workings of Yorkshire pits. Down below two other lads and myself were sent with a German worker to empty tubs of waste stone salts and we were expected to tip the tubs over sideways to empty them. As I looked at them, I realized that each single tub must have reached at least a ton. I had only just recovered from my wounds and, although I didn't know the extent of the other prisoners' injuries, I knew that I hadn't the strength to help move them. It would have been much simpler to run them forward on the lines at speed and tip them up endways.

It vexed the German so much to see that we couldn't move it that, in his temper, he lashed out at us with his fist and caught me with a beauty, so much that I was dumped on my backside. This action was senseless but fortunately I saw a length of timber which could solve our problem. I asked the lads to fetch it and fixed it under the centre of the tub to cantilever the weight and with very little effort on our part we overturned the first tub. . . . The German then shouted something and by signs, the same in any language, he pointed his fingers to his open mouth. Then he set off to where his snack was kept and the other two followed. I went to pick up my acetylene lamp and en route had to pass an open gate where the shot firers had been drilling. Just then a blast took place, blew my lamp out and I was in total darkness. After tumbling against the tubs and regularly tripping over lines and sleepers, I was thankful eventually to see a glimmer from an electric bulb. What a feeling of relief! I had visions of wandering in these caverns for ever.

One prisoner who experienced more than his share of camps, with their varying standards and attitudes, was Lieutenant Cecil Blain of the RFC, who was captured when his aircraft was forced down over Maubeuge in August 1916. Having spent some time in filthy cells at Cambrai, he was taken to Gütersloh,, where:

After a hot bath and good sleep in clean surroundings we all, I think, felt much better. The quarantine building was separate from the main camp and divided into two. After a few days in one half we were moved into the other, where we met a lot more who had been captured a few days previous to us. After a week or so here we were all moved into the main camp. It held about 1,000 officers, British, French, Belgian and Russian. They nearly all had been captured very early in the war and were very pleased to hear all we had to tell them. Here, thanks to the untiring efforts of the American Ambassador, we were able to live more or less in comparative comfort, being able to get out of sight of the Boche.

One could get a fair amount of sport, such as tennis, hockey, football, etc., and with this and the kindness of our fellow prisoners in giving us food etc., we soon picked up what we had lost at Cambrai. We were not to stay here long, however, for towards the end of September all the newly captured flying officers were warned for another camp. So on a certain fine day in September, after a splendid send-off, twenty-eight of us boarded a train for Osnabrück.

Here we were again searched and packed into rooms where all the windows were whitewashed and no-one was allowed to see out. We were allowed little or no exercise at all, and were told we were in quarantine. We were kept under these conditions for about three weeks, all the windows being locked. We were allowed to write one letter a day during this period instead of the usual two and four post-cards a month which seemed rather unusual. Eventually, however, the truth leaked out that we had been sent here to be shot as a reprisal of some sort. At the end of three weeks we were questioned separately by a detective and let loose into the camp where we met a lot more Russian and French officers, together with one Englishman and a French flying officer (really a Maltese) about whom you will hear more later on.

The amount of exercise to be got in this camp was really very small. However boxing and wrestling were started, and as more and more Englishmen arrived we managed to make the best of everything. Parcels and letters came better here than in any other camp I was in, being the main depot for the censoring of letters for the 10th Army Corps, a Hanover Command, but things did not continue to run smoothly. The General in command started to make a name for himself as a real bully, taking advantage of his position on every possible occasion, and things went from bad to worse as all our complaints as to sanitary conditions etc. were unheeded. It was at this camp that escape really entered my head as a necessary form of action, so with two others, plans were made. . . .

We waited a few days and got ready again for the last time. Opposite the window we were to escape from was a small room occupied by the Maltese Capitaine Allouche. He was a dirty brute, distrusted and disliked by all, and we had been warned about him by the French officers. He gave us away, for the next morning the great General and about six Huns walked into our rooms and held a search. They got practically everything and it was all put down in my name, for which I went to the jug.

Blain and his colleagues had their revenge on Allouche; they smothered him in treacle and ashes and anything else they could lay their hands on. As a result, the English officers were removed from Osnabrück and taken to Clausthal in the Harz Mountains. On arrival, they were taken before the commandant, who told them that they were to be court-martialled for their unruly behaviour. They had two French colonels for their defence, but to no avail; the court martial, which was held in Hanover, was clearly rigged, and their punishment had already been fixed at 500 marks each or fifty days. Blain continues:

When we arrived at Clausthal station with all our belongings – pots and pans dangling from sticks over our shoulders – at about 10.30 p.m., we could not go to the camp that night, we were told, and would have a sleep on the station. Our mouths dropped, for there was two foot of snow on the ground [it was now the winter of 1916–17] but we soon cheered up when we were shown into the most luxurious waiting room, where soup, ham and bread were served to us, and we were told that by signing our names in a book we could get all the wine etc. we wanted. What a night! I won't go into detail, but it was a very happy-looking crowd that wended its way uphill through deep snow carrying our own baggage to camp. . . . There were a lot more English there, but we were not wanted. They all wore masses of clothes, looked unhappy, and informed us in polite language that it was not a good place. However, it was a palace to us after the last camp. There were two squash courts, a tennis court, and tobogganing inside the camp. We should get really fit here, we thought, but it was 200 miles to the frontier. . . .

The house was a very temporary-looking structure made of cement and wood, and after a time heating was only allowed in the huge dining-room by radiation. Coal was scarce and so was light. However, we made ourselves a bit more comfortable here than before and settled down to make fresh plans for escape. There were, besides the house, two barracks, and under each of these tunnels were started, both of which I worked in for some time, but eventually got tired of them and decided to make our exit by another route.

After an abortive escape attempt, and six weeks in the cells, Blain was transferred to the camp at Ströhen near Hanover – 'one of the very worst that existed'. He was there for a fortnight and then moved again, this time to Neuenkirchen in Westphalia, which he described as 'a wonderful place, quite new. No-one knew the slightest thing about running a camp, and we had some very amusing scenes. Someone worked out that it took seventy-six sentries to keep forty in this camp.'

Meanwhile, in the mining camps of Silesia, the misery went on, and in 1917 privation was beginning to have its effect on German civilian workers as well as on the POWs. This is illustrated by the diary of Cpl Green of the Scots Guards, which records that 22 January 1917

was absolutely the most sensational day of our period of 'visiting' Germany. We were on the day shift 6 a.m. till 2 p.m. At the end of the shift when number 4 district were waiting to go up, their Oberhauer [foreman] suddenly attacked young 'Jinny' Holland with his pick. For what reason, is not known. Steel, another Englishman, duly came up and gripped the Pole's arms in defence of Holland, when a third man, unknown, but surmised to be Russian, came up and hit the Pole on the head with his lamp, and much blood flew round. It was only just starting, for the overseer came to assist his boss, but he was given a beautiful jab in the left eye by Parfitt, the third Englishman. His eye was about the best I have ever seen for size.

Things quietened down now and the men were duly up, washed and changed. Then the three Englishmen were called by the old German sentry, who said the bathmaster wanted to see them. Naturally they went, but when they got to the outside door Steel told them to keep their eyes open. They were taken down not to the bathman but to the civilian bathhouse instead. Here the over bosses awaited them, picks in hand. The door was locked upon them. Not a move was made until Steiger Wilkie began the attack. Holland stopped the first blow on the crown of his head, and then managed to escape from them and came up to tell us what was happening. The tall Polish sentry was in our bath house talking to Ward when he heard the shouts of Steel and Parfitt being attacked. He immediately came up and went through to their assistance, but it was all finished before he got there. The two were knocked absolutely unconscious.

The terrible reverses suffered by Romania in her battles against the invading armies of Germany and Austria-Hungary during the latter half of 1916 led to a massive influx of Romanian prisoners into the POW camps in the east; like the Russians, the Romanians endured fearful hardships. Many thousands were concentrated in Lamsdorf, also in Silesia, alongside French, Russians, Serbians, and about 2,000 British. At the beginning of 1917, at least ten Romanians in Lamsdorf were dying each day from cold and starvation. To make room for the Romanians, about 1,000 Russians were transferred to Schneidemühl from Lamsdorf; three hundred of them died from cold and hunger before the transfer could take place.

At Langensalza in Thuringia, where the POWs were also compelled to work in nearby mines, their lot seems to have been somewhat better than that of their counterparts in Silesia. Private R. Preston of the KRRC records that in 1917

> The time between bed and work was spent by trying not to be bored to death and we were grateful that the sergeant would bring us practically anything we required. I asked him to bring me a good translation booklet for English and German and he brought me an 'Otto Onions' Lehrer. . . . We all clubbed together for a hand-wound gramaphone and the sergeant brought us the

best of Viennese records and opera songs together with a pack of playing cards. The difficulty was keeping the music going whilst playing cards because the gramaphone could only play one record at each winding. We solved that problem by engaging one of the men who was a bit sub standard and applauding him each time he put a good record on. We declared that we'd never heard anyone play a record so well, much to his obvious pleasure. This man came in handy for looking after the stove and cooking us a rice pudding in an enamel bowl when we found that we had accumulated sufficient rice and a couple of tins of milk from our parcels.

Some Sundays we would be taken to the Lutheran Church in the village on Saint days. We were also marched up to the village when our parcels were due to arrive. Once we were even taken to a village fete in a wooded valley where a German band played for the people to dance and enjoy themselves. There we were allowed to sit and watch and drink our beer in peace. But this happened only once and it was a very sad day for us when we learnt that our sergeant was to be transferred to other duties. A Bavarian sergeant took his place and he was a different type of person altogether.

Nevertheless, there were compensations at Langensalza. The prisoners were in daily contact with German women who worked in the salt-mines to earn workers' food rations and any surplus goods which were issued to the mine-workers. Many prisoners were befriended by these women – an understandable turn of events, given the fact that the surrounding area was virtually devoid of able-bodied German males.

Security at Langensalza was not particularly tight, as Preston relates:

The view over our sleeping barracks showed a wood consisting of about a square mile of massive beech trees . . . from the mine towards where the village lay was a thirty-foot Riding, more of a fire break and used as a green road. I could see our exercise yard surrounded with wire fencing – it was fifty yards square with toilet and washing trough. Away from the end of the beech trees a large patch of shrub grew which made good cover. On the right of the Riding there was a pine forest which stretched for miles and hid the village in the valley. . . . By climbing the wire at the end of the building I could just manage to get my backside on to the eaves of one of the huts and slide down to the soft bushes. ... From then on every Sunday I put my German book under my jacket, took cover in secret, crossed the Riding after making sure no-one was about and scurried into the pine forest to sit and read in the beautiful fresh air and sunshine before returning to the camp.

In 1915, an investigative committee, presided over by Lord Justice Younger, was set up to compile a report on the conditions inside the German POW camps. Its work went on throughout the period of hostilities, during which time it examined the evidence of nearly 4,000 British officers and men who had either escaped or been repatriated. The findings of the committee were reasonably accurate, although they tended to concentrate on officer POW camps. In this respect, the committee was scathing in its condemnation of conditions in four camps, all under the jurisdiction of a General von Hänisch; these were at Clausthal, Ströhen, Schwarmstedt, and Holzminden.

Of Clausthal, situated 2,000 feet above sea-level in the Harz mountains, the report stated:

The dining-room was disgracefully overcrowded, dirty and filthy. ... It was inadequate for officers [120] living in the hotel, and its utter incapacity may be realized when to that number a further 130 from the huts are added. It was quite impossible for the orderlies to keep the place clean. First, it was the only place available where the officers could sit and read, work, smoke or play cards, chess, etc. Secondly, the officers, in messes of from two to six, had to prepare their food here for cooking. Thirdly, the orderlies had to use it as a scullery to clean up not only crockery and cutlery, but pots and pans as well.

A form of collective punishment repeatedly used in this camp was to close the lower half of the grounds. An alternative once employed during two winter months was to deny light in the bedrooms, thereby compelling officers to sit in a freezingly cold room in the dark from, say, 5 p.m. to nearly 10 p.m. – five whole hours – when the lights were turned on for a few minutes. Complaints were made of the sanitation in the camp, and the washing arrangements were insufficient. After August, 1917, there were walks on parole at the rate of a walk to each officer every six weeks.

The tone of the camp will be understood from the methods of a man like Niemeyer, the commandant, who encouraged guards to shoot. 'An officer . . . having dropped his cap from a window, jumped out to pick it up, and although not in the five yards [neutral zone] was fired at by the sentry, who fortunately missed.'

The quarters which had been sufficient for punishments at the beginning of the camp's history had been one cell, 'a small room . . . next door to the pig-sty on two sides, and to the electric motor-house on the other, a most foul place'. It was abandoned in consequence of the protest of the officers, but 'on the arrival of General von Hänisch, the latter gave instructions that it should be used, and was good enough for the English'. Later, it was replaced by a hut completed towards the end of June, 1917, which contained 16 cells or more. These, henceforward, were always full, except for some kept empty for officers who attempted to escape.

Ströhen, as the committee's report stated, was even worse:

The camp at Ströhen Moor was some two acres in extent. It comprised three large, two medium, and three smaller wooden huts or sheds, a hospital, dining and reading hut – all in a bad state of repair – within a double barbed wire square enclosure, the whole situated in the midst of four swamps. In the centre lay two stagnant pools. On the east side of the camp, close to the trench latrine, the foul condition of which was a continuous infliction on the prisoners, were two pumps, one with fresh water of indifferent quality, and the other with water of a dark colour. The camp in wet weather was a morass; in hot weather a place of dust-storms and stench.

Ströhen, it is said, had been a camp where Russian and Romanian officers had been treated with exceptional severity. Its commandant, Major von Kichton, was a savage man, unrestrained either by feeling or reason. The attitude adopted by the guards throughout the period when von Kichton was commandant, and during the six weeks subsequent to his departure when Hauptmann Niemeyer, afterwards commandant at Holzminden, succeeded him, was uniformly threatening. [This Niemeyer was the twin brother of the commandant at Clausthal, and equally unpleasant.] The cells were always full, while a long list of officers sentenced awaited their turn for confinement. Punishment was given on the word of a guard without appeal, and with the most arbitrary indifference to justice, as when a teetotaller was sentenced for drunkenness, or an officer was shut up for an offence of which a comrade admitted himself to be the author. No reason was given for the denial of this slight solace for prisoners penned up in a camp too small for customary exercise.

At Schwarmstedt, the attitude of the guards was not too bad, but the living conditions were deplorable.

Schwarmstedt camp is situated on the main Lüneberger Heide, north-east of the river Aller, about seven miles from the town of that name. Within an area of four and a half acres it included three dormitory huts, one canteen and dining-room hut, and two smaller huts for officers. It contained 400 officer prisoners and 80 orderlies. Before May, 1917, it had been occupied by Romanian officers, still earlier by Russian prisoners. Like Ströhen, the camp was a quagmire in wet weather. The drinking water had a bad colour, taste, and smell, the sanitation was deplorable, the light defective. There were no adequate washing arrangements; the German food was offensively cooked, and, except during the first fortnight, when there were no parcels, it was usually left untouched, when, even the hungry guards refusing to eat it, it was given to the pigs. The buildings leaked, and the prisoners were crowded together. In addition, the camp was exceptionally dirty.

The prison was kept full, with a waiting list of officers sentenced but not punished. There were the endless appells and queues, and oppressive searches. Yet the commandant was not thought to be actively malicious or revengeful. 'Colonel von Diest did his best to make things as bearable as he could for us; for example, he had a parcel room built and several stoves installed, but his attempts were in nearly every case frustrated by General von Hänisch.' The non-commissioned officers, who at first shouted at the prisoners, quickly behaved themselves more correctly towards them. Thus life at Schwarmstedt was not a constant suffering. While the soil of the camp did not lend itself to games, free walks on parole were allowed and enjoyed. These facilities were later much curtailed from headquarters, and

General von Hänisch himself prohibited the use of the swimming bath.

Holzminden's main drawbacks, it appeared, were overcrowding and a lack of recreational facilities.

The buildings, which were new, were composed of two barracks, in one of which was installed the administration of the camp with the guard; in the other, the orderlies, in addition to the officer prisoners. The space was by this disposition crowded to excess. The indoor conditions were also particularly unfavourable for sociable occupations. There were no common rooms, no space in which to study, hold classes, or give entertainments. Officers were obliged, therefore, to pass much of their time in the overcrowded, unfurnished, and unheated sleeping-rooms. The only sitting-rooms were, as at Clausthal, the dining-rooms of the barracks. Officers suffered besides from the lack of appliances for washing, but the camp was better provided in this regard and in that of sanitation than in any of the others in the Hanover command.

The prison cells, which were always full, in the cellars of the barracks, were most unsuitable. There were no sanitary arrangements in connexion with them, and it is said that the food of imprisoned officers was served out on the floor of the space on which were placed the make-shift latrines. Another hardship at Holzminden was particularly severe for British officers, the absence of recreation. Football was forbidden within the camp area; hockey equally was almost impossible, for the ground was too small, though it might easily have been enlarged. All that remained was the opportunity of taking walks in the neighbourhood, but here, owing to General von Hänisch's action, the walks were interrupted till February, 1918.

Naturally, conditions in the camps varied according to the numbers of prisoners confined in them, and this was very much a fluctuating value. In the first two years of the war 29,297 prisoners, mostly Russians and including 6,270 who succumbed later to wounds received in action, died in German POW camps, but by mid-1916 the number of prisoners still in confinement still totalled 1,646,233. Of these, 1,200,000 were Russians, 355,000 French 40,000 British, and the remainder Serbs and other nationalities. The total, it should be mentioned, does not include 45,000 civilian internees. The Battle of Cambrai in November added another 9,000 British officers and men to the POW population.

Worse was to come. The German spring offensives of 1918 were to result in the capture of more British troops than had been taken prisoner during the whole of the previous three years. The British armies bore the brunt of the onslaught, and before the end of May close on 100,000 men were marching into captivity.

Chapter 4

CIVILIAN INTERNEES

Of all the targets for British propaganda during the 1914–18 war, few received more consistent attention than the civilian internment camp at Ruhleben, where internees, according to the popular Press, were regularly subjected to a variety of 'horrors and tortures'. This was quite untrue. Although lacking many amenities, Ruhleben was a place in which several thousand British civilian prisoners and thousands more foreign nationals survived adequately, if not in comfort, 'for the duration'.

Ruhleben was an improvised camp built on a racecourse near Berlin, and eventually became the headquarters camp for nearly all British civilian prisoners, of whom there were about 6,000, all males of military age. Most had been rounded up by the end of November 1914. Predominantly, they were men who had been employed in Germany, although some were captured in the occupied territories of France and Belgium. At Ruhleben they were quartered in stables, lofts, and other buildings. The first few months were the most uncomfortable, but as time went by conditions were gradually improved.

One of Ruhleben's inmates was Percy Brown, a free-lance photographer accredited to the *London Graphic*. While on an assignment in Holland he inadvertently crossed the German border, was arrested, and for a time, until he convinced the German authorities otherwise, risked being shot as a spy. He wrote:

> To me Ruhleben was a rest cure. Here time stood still, no days or weeks to portion off the indefinite stretch. If you happened to pass the YMCA building, Sunday was faintly marked by the devout droning of hymns, a pause, a shuffling of feet after a prayer, and

then the slow exit of prisoners breaking off into groups to discuss the sermon, just as in any English village.

But there was also much to see inside and outside the barbed wire. Trains packed with soldiers and guns passed to Germany's several fronts every few moments, night and day, on the military railway which ran alongside the camp. The cheering troops decorated themselves and their guns with signs, 'Nach Paris', 'Nach London', and foliage from the country they had just been battering. No sign of foliage or gaiety was noticed after the second year. The troops sat silent and weary in the open trucks staring enviously at us in our guarded safety. Occasionally a trainload of British soldiers fresh from the Western Front cheered and shouted good news to us as they passed on their way to the terrible prison camps.

Thanks to the British Government and relatives we were the best-fed prisoners. No matter how many ships were sunk we got our parcels. It is true one sailor was shocked while slicing a loaf of mouldy bread; he had cut through a nest of mice. But that was exceptional. The British Government installed bakeries in Holland, from which we received long loaves of white bread. We had everything which could be got into a can. Our industrious gardeners supplied us with vegetables in season, such as tomatoes, onions, beans, cabbage, marrows and beetroot, and everyone, whether English, pro-German, or, in some cases, pure-German, could draw a dole from our Government.

Most things could be purchased in Ruhleben, although the price was often high; in 1916, for example, the price of an English newspaper was three pounds. In many respects, restrictions in Ruhleben were harsher than those in Stadtvogtei, the Berlin prison in which some internees – usually those suspected of spying – had been incarcerated; there, although it was against the rules, they could obtain what they wanted – newspapers, meat, eggs, coffee, whisky, kitchen and even photographic equipment – simply by handing a list and money to a friendly soldier-warder. In Ruhleben, although internees were able to buy useful items such as mirrors, paper, shaving tackle, and vegetables in season, certain items were prohibited. Alcohol was rigidly banned, with the exception of ersatz beer that could be obtained in the Casino and wine sold at extortionate prices by one of the German officers, who opened a bar under the main grandstand and charged fourpence a glass. Despite this sum, which was outrageous for the time, the wine was good and provided a degree of comfort, so that the wine queue became longer and more popular than any other in the camp. It was also a convenient rendezvous where internees could exchange the latest rumours, gossip, and war news.

Trade was so good that the German officer decided to increase the price to sixpence a glass. The demand continued unabated and so did the price rises, until eventually a glass of wine cost three shillings and ninepence. That was too much for everyone except a handful, and the wine queue shortened dramatically. 'Only the rich and rough-necks remained,' says Brown.

It was a curious sight to see well-groomed British merchants taking wine with some of the meanest thugs who ever stole a sick prisoner's parcel. Many of the gang bought their wine with money made by selling presents from old ladies at home who had adopted what they thought were lonely destitute prisoners. Each man could get himself adopted by as many senders as he cared to write to. Lists of good-natured people were sent to the camp which the gang exploited, and they also got their names on every charitable society list. The scandal grew until one man got as many as thirty parcels a day. Then a central parcels committee took control, and no matter how many parcels were sent to rich and crafty prisoners, everyone received exactly the same amount.

As was the case in POW camps, the internees depended on parcels for their principal supply of food; the German rations were inadequate and usually only the potatoes were accepted. The only recorded time when the internees demanded their full ration issue was as a reprisal. It happened when the camp commandant gave a speech to the assembled internees, laying heavy emphasis on German gains and British losses. As his speech ended, there was a loud raspberry from the crowd and the German imperial ensign went fluttering down from its mast into the mud, its halyard cut by an irate British sailor. As a result, all the internees were confined to barracks for a week. As a reprisal, four thousand internees marched on the camp kitchens, chanting and demanding their full ration allowance, beating time with tin plates. The guards were powerless, the kitchen staff was unable to cope, and the CB order was quickly lifted.

57

In 1917, with U-boats taking a heavy toll of Allied shipping, Ruhleben experienced a serious food shortage for a period of several weeks. According to Percy Brown, even the bread from Holland did not arrive, and hardly anything remained in the internees' cupboards. The camp racketeers, many of whom had hoarded food against just this kind of emergency, did a roaring trade. Even so, the internees continued to spurn the German rations – with the exception of potatoes and rice – and existed on what they could scrape together until the parcels began to arrive once more.

The only real plague which threatened Ruhleben, Brown recounts, was rats.

Hunger drove them from Berlin, and scores could be seen near the parcel vans scenting the bacon. We had a colony of big dark brutes under our barracks. They ate holes in the floor between the beds. We did not worry about them but listened to their gnawings and squeaks.

By the dim light we could make out their shadowy bodies about the floor. They seemed to work with a human understanding. One worked below the boards and another from above. Jerry [Jerry Lane, a lace-machine maker from St Quentin] had had experience of rat plague in the north of France. He said if the camp was not cleared of the pests they would breed so fast they would eat us alive after they had finished our food. Jerry said they talked. Rats passed the word from colony to colony during famines, which takes some believing!

One night I woke with a start. Someone had put a finger on my face, I thought. I could see nothing, but heard the usual noises of the rats. In the morning when Jerry went to the cupboard for the bacon it was missing, also a big piece of cheese. I suspected thieves, but he assured me that a team of rats could remove articles heavier than themselves. We boarded up the hole, but it was gnawed away again.

Our most precious food, the occasional eggs, also disappeared. A rat as big as a rabbit ran along the top of Jerry's bunk, showing his teeth and diving into the darkness. The pests began to worry us. As they increased they became savage and determined, not vanishing when seen. In fact they glared at us hungrily.

Our saviour was Dr Jephson, who got permission for the prisoners to own dogs. He organized a rat hunt. All sorts of dogs and men turned out and joined Jephson. He went to the root of the trouble. Attached to every barrack was a refuse bin about thirty feet long, which made safe cover for the pests. A gang was put to work to dig out the accumulated refuse. More than a score of big rats were killed in the first half-hour. The brutes screamed and fought back fiercely, and several dogs were withdrawn from the hunt.

Every bit of cover was removed and disinfectant placed on the floor. This was done with the bins of the twenty-odd barracks. Hundreds of rats were killed during a campaign lasting weeks. Not until half the camp had been hunted did the rats seem to decrease. When the bins and drains were clear the rats were seen to lurk outside the wire waiting for night. Jephson went further and got permission to take the pack outside to hunt the area round the camp. Finally, after weeks of systematic searching, he destroyed the enemy.

But officially the plague persisted. Long after we had seen the last rat the doctor continued his meets, which started in 'Bond Street', our shopping street. The hunt grew, men and dogs, now that the operations went on outside the camp. There were wonderful drives into the neighbourhood, of course accompanied by armed guards, who also developed an enthusiasm for rat hunting. There were lots of things to do once out of sight of the windows of the offices. Rats became very scarce and it was a job to show results. When a few were caught some had to be kept back to show for slack days. In fact, when things were very bad we had to buy a few rats to keep the hunt going. When the doctor began to include Charlottenburg, a mile away, in his drives, and the crowd of hunt followers increased, the authorities judged that the danger was past and cancelled the permits.

Thanks to the efforts of the camp doctors and the co-operation of the German authorities, outbreaks of disease in the crowded conditions of Ruhleben were kept to a minimum. Once, in 1917, there was a serious outbreak of dysentery which affected practically the whole camp and resulted in three deaths; it occurred when a large shipment of steak was condemned as unfit by the sanitary authorities in Berlin and, either by design or accident, was issued to Ruhleben. As Percy Brown reported:

We marched to the kitchens in barrack formation, and collected a piece of meat each. And the meat tasted good. That evening several were taken ill. By ten o'clock half the camp had made a journey to 'Spandau' [the latrines area] in acute agony. At midnight the place was crowded and in filthy overflow. Men sitting at their tables were suddenly taken short in terrible agony, and had to race away, only to collapse on the way to the lavatories. Their box-mates had to carry them to the bath-house to be washed and have their clothes changed. . . . The occasion brought out the best from those unaffected. They washed and changed the clothes of the victims night and day until the epidemic had spent itself, the most unpleasant job one man could do for another.

Internees who suffered serious illness were sent for treatment to Schönungs Barracke, a military establishment in the Berlin suburbs; a small hospital was set up there in 1915 by a group of internees under the guidance of a Mr Lambert, who appears to have worked tirelessly on behalf of the sick but about whom, unfortunately, history records little more than his surname. Later, patients were allowed to spend time in a sanatorium while they recuperated; this establishment was run by a Dr Weiler, and patients had to pay fees.

A curious kind of apartheid existed in Ruhleben. Coloured internees, no matter what their nationality, were accommodated in a communal barracks, so that Sikhs rubbed shoulders with Africans and Malays. The majority were merchant seamen, interned in German ports on the outbreak of war or captured on the high seas by commerce raiders. Despite powerful ethnic and religious differences, they got on well together and visits to their barracks provided a rich source of entertainment, for many of them were accomplished musicians. Also, for a small fee, they would undertake menial tasks for the other internees; as Percy Brown says, 'Joe, a Kru "boy" of sixty years, who had been rescued from a torpedoed ship, washed up and made delicious curry for us.'

They did these jobs without complaint, and the other internees were high in their praise of them. Brown describes their barracks as

the happiest and cleanest in the camp. Most of the coloured men played, sang and danced. Their life was a continuous concert. . . . West Indians and Malays played lullabies in undertones, quiet, soothing music with no banging or discord. In the centre of the barracks was a laughing laundry firm of five Africans. As they ironed out the wash they hummed lilting spirituals to the strokes of the irons. At the back entrance our cobbler danced a queer little rhythmic dance to the singing tone of the ukelele while half a dozen customers waited patiently for their clogs.

Brown records that disputes were rare in the coloured internees' barracks.

If a young negro became overheated in the wine line, the old men would calm him and tell him to keep out of the white men's troubles. Some did not care who won the war so long as it was finished quickly and they could go back to their own hot climates.

Meanwhile, they looked after their health. Several had their native herbal medicines sent by relatives all the way from their native countries. They made regular use of the bath-houses, being very particular about their skins, which they scrubbed and rubbed with oils. On dark winter mornings their bronze bodies were invisible to us until they had covered themselves with foaming lather which made them look like ghosts. Then with a laugh they would turn on the ice-cold shower and stand rubbing themselves until every trace of soap was washed away.

If some of Brown's remarks sound a little patronizing, it should be remembered that during this period the customs and habits of peoples of non-European stock were not generally familiar to Europeans, unless they had served in the colonies; it must have come as quite a culture shock to discover that Africans and Asians, viewed from a position of enforced equality rather than from the pedestal of Empire, were kindly, decent, and generally intelligent folk. What the coloured internees thought about the white inmates of Ruhleben is, unfortunately, not recorded.

Chapter 5

THE RED CROSS AND RELIEF ORGANIZATIONS

Despite the chaos and confusion that attended the great battles on the eastern and western fronts in 1914–15, and the lack of accurate information – at least in the early months – on millions of men, the machinery of the International Committee of the Red Cross geared up with truly remarkable speed and efficiency to meet the needs of war prisoners of all the belligerents. The Red Cross had been authorized by a diplomatic conference, held in Washington in 1912, to act as official intermediary in aiding prisoners of war; on the outbreak of hostilities in August 1914 its first act was to set up a Central Agency for this purpose. With its headquarters in Geneva, the Agency was subdivided into sections to cater for the needs of the various belligerent nations; the British Section, for example, had a staff of eighty-three, working in shifts around the clock.

All these sections worked within the framework of four principal departments. One was responsible for compiling information about POWs and passing on news of their whereabouts to their families; the second dealt with letters, parcels, and money; the third was responsible for supervising conditions in the POW camps on both sides; and the fourth dealt with repatriation and the welfare of internees in neutral countries.

The first, most immediate, and most formidable task was to obtain lists of prisoners from all the belligerents. Some nations – notably the Germans – were efficient in transmitting this vital information; others, particularly the Russians, were not. Nevertheless, a massive catalogue of POWs and their whereabouts was slowly built up, and as the names came in the Central Agency began the laborious task of compiling a card index. The administrative workload was enormous; eventually, the typing pool alone occupied a hundred women, working full-time. A standard information card was also produced and issued to the belligerent governments; on it, prisoners were asked to fill in essential details – name, rank, home address, POW camp address, and so on. To give some idea of the work involved, the French Section alone generated two and a half million of these cards, the German Section one and a half million and the British Section 500,000. Early in 1915 a Civil Department was also created to cater for foreign nationals living in countries which had suddenly become enemies of their own states.

All these activities were undertaken in close co-operation with prisoners-of-war information bureaux set up by the belligerent governments. One such bureau was established in London within a week of the outbreak of hostilities; its headquarters were at Wellington Street, in the Strand, not far from Covent Garden. It was directed by a senior Civil Servant, Sir Paul Harvey, who recruited an expert staff from various Civil Service departments; he was succeeded in the post by Sir J. D. Rees in 1915. From relatively small beginnings, the bureau expanded gradually during the war years until it had a staff of 300 or more.

The principal task of the bureau was to maintain a complete register of all alien enemies who were interned in any part of the British Empire. POW and internment camp commandants were required to provide a list of all new prisoners as soon as possible after their arrival; this was later supplemented by more detailed returns, compiled with the aid of Red Cross information cards. Copies of these returns were constantly updated and transmitted via Geneva to the German, Austrian, and Bulgarian Red Cross Societies, and to the Ottoman Red Crescent Society. The bureau also handled details of sick and wounded prisoners in British POW camps; commandants forwarded regular returns of prisoners admitted to and discharged from hospital, and this information was sent on to enemy governments so that relatives and friends could be kept informed. Another department of the bureau had the grim task of compiling returns of enemy dead from information received from GHQ, these particulars being accompanied, wherever possible, by identity discs and personal effects. These, again, were forwarded to the families of the dead via Geneva. At the height of the war, the London bureau was dealing with as many as 400 enquiries every day concerning the welfare of German prisoners alone.

By the end of 1914, a massive parcel traffic had begun to flow to the camps of Europe. In Britain, parcel-packing for POWs was initiated at the various regimental depots under the initial auspices of the Church Army, which provided large numbers of volunteers. Parcels were sent not only to British but also to Russian POWs, who did not have the benefit of similar welfare organizations and whose plight in the winter of 1914–15 was desperate. In an attempt to centralize the efforts of the various volunteer groups a Prisoners of War Help Committee was formed, but it failed to achieve the desired result – mainly because it received little official backing – and eventually the food supply organization was taken over by the Red Cross. In the early months of the war, with prisoners being transferred from camp to camp in order to make room for new batches, the parcel traffic was erratic, but as time went by and administration improved with experience it settled down into a more efficient routine and most camps received regular supplies. For most of the war the main parcel collection and distribution centre was Berne, although at a later date some of the work was undertaken by the Red Cross in Copenhagen. In Britain, the central depot for parcel-packing and onward transmission, once the Red Cross had assumed full control, was Thurloe Place in South Kensington, where 750 people were employed in this task. The aim was to provide each prisoner with one 10 lb parcel and 13 lb of bread every fortnight. For the Swiss, it was business on a grand scale: one Geneva-based haulage firm alone, appointed by the Red Cross, handled two million POW parcels between September 1914 and November 1918.

A very good description of the parcel distribution system in a POW camp, and of what the parcels generally contained, was given by Captain McMurtrie of the Somerset Light Infantry, who in the spring of 1918 was in Graudenz.

Once the parcels and letters began to come regularly we were all right, especially as large consignments of shirts, socks, pyjamas etc were sent by the Red Cross. Meanwhile, a large number of cases of biscuits and 'emergency' parcels were also sent to the camp by the Red Cross. If any officer did not get a food parcel for a week then he was given one of these emergency parcels. The biscuits were ordinary hard biscuits which were kept as a reserve in case the frontiers were closed (as they were for about a month, once or twice a year) and thus we still had food to carry on with even though our parcels had stopped coming. Later as more food came into the camp we gave a great many biscuits to the French officers' camp at Graudenz who were badly in need of food.

The procedure for parcels was as follows: One English officer and three English privates went down to the post office each day with a guard. There they picked up the parcels and the officer checked the numbers. When the parcels got to the camp, they were immediately taken to the 'parcel house', a small building with about six small rooms in it. Here they were unloaded and the parcels for half the officers in the camp went to the 'right' rooms and the other half to the 'left'. They were all set out in order, numbered, and then the number was put against the officer's name on a printed list which was posted on the notice boards.

The next day those officers for whom parcels had come would queue up in the required 'margarine style' queue and would get their parcels in alphabetical order. There was always a German officer, one or two sergeant majors and four German privates watching. The parcel was opened and all tinned goods were put in the officer's tin locker (every officer had a tin locker in the parcel house.) The number of tins would be entered in a book. The rest of the parcel the officer could take away unless there was some forbidden article, which would be confiscated. In the case of clothes, all civilian clothes were either kept by the Huns until the Armistice was signed or, if the officer wished, broad stripes were sewn into the clothes. All clothes parcels were carefully searched by the Boche before being passed.

Candles, compasses and books were kept by the Boche. Books were censored and then returned. There were about eight English officers in each room doing the work and running everything to do with parcels. The Boche simply cleared away the rubbish and saw or did not see that tins were not taken out unopened. Tins were not allowed to be taken away unopened; I suppose for fear of compasses etc being hidden in them. Once or twice a day, officers could draw their tins. They came with plates and stated their locker number and the tins would be opened and deposited on their plates. Needless to say, all these queues were a constant source of annoyance. There were many exciting moments when officers, with the assistance of confederates inside the parcel room, would get their parcels out whole or tins out unopened. If an officer knew that a parcel contained something that could be used to assist escape, it was smuggled out.

The food that we were given was ample to live on; however, as soon as we had got over our starvation period and were used to food, the continual tinned food, tinned everything, began to get on our nerves. There is something about the ordinary tinned food which you cannot get away from, unless you have flavouring and we had none.

From our Red Cross parcels we got Quaker Oats, tea, milk, cocoa, bully, maconochie cheese, biscuits, jam, marmalade, tinned puddings, milk puddings, margarine, potted meat, bacon and sugar; but all of it tasted of tins. We also received at first white bread, which was mouldy, but at that time we were too hungry to throw it away. Later we received boxes of hard biscuits from Berne and towards the end white bread was once more sent which was quite fresh. Hopkins also had a parcel of about 14 eggs, 1 lb butter and 1 lb cheese every week so we were well supplied.

The efforts of the Red Cross undoubtedly prevented many thousands of Allied prisoners from starving to death during those terrible years of 1914–18. But the Red Cross was at the apex of a huge pyramid of effort that encompassed many other voluntary agencies, and none of the results achieved would have been possible without a quite remarkable degree of efficiency on the part of the transport and postal authorities in the countries concerned. But at the grass-roots of all the effort were the prisoners' welfare associations formed by the various regiments, and a good description of the work of one of them is given by Major John Ewing, MC, in his *Regimental History of the Royal Scots, 1914–19* (Edinburgh: Oliver & Boyd, 1925).

The hardest worked fund of all was the Prisoners' Fund. Previous to November 1916 food for prisoners was provided in a somewhat irregular manner by private individuals, who were permitted to go into any shop or store and send parcels to their friends. During this period the Royal Scots Association secured several hundreds of subscribers, who transmitted parcels to prisoners in a more or less irregular way. The absence of system led to abuses and overlapping, and in November 1916 the authorities enacted that Regimental Care Committees should be formed, through whom alone parcels should be sent to prisoners. The Royal Scots Association was the first in Scotland to set up a Regimental Care Committee, which regularly forwarded three parcels per fortnight to each prisoner connected with the Regiment. The work involved was enormous, and large sums of money were required to defray the expenses incurred on behalf of the vast number of prisoners (which in 1918, in the case of the Royal Scots, amounted to 84 officers and 2,283 other ranks) for whom the Care Committee was responsible. Appeals to the public were issued, signed by Lord Rosebery, who had always taken an active interest in the Regiment, by the Lord Provost, and by the Chairman of the Royal Scots Association, Lord Salvesen, with the result that within the regimental district the sum of £62,000 was collected. . . .

Large as was the sum raised by subscription it did not avail to meet the needs of the Regiment, but no prisoners, were ever neglected, owing to the patriotism of the officials of the Association, who used their private means to make up deficiencies. It was ascertained that the upkeep of each man required £36 per year, and that the total annual cost of supplying prisoners with food amounted to 1s 6d per head of the total population of the regimental district. In many cases the work of the Care Committee was lightened by the generous action of individual citizens who made themselves responsible for supplying the wants of a number of prisoners. The 'adopters', as they were called, not only provided for the cost of one or more of these men, but kept up a correspondence with them which did much to relieve the gloom of their captivity.

The Committee was helped enormously by a large and patriotic band of voluntary workers. The depot, where goods were stored, was at 20 Royal Circus, and three times a week the staff of packers and other workers sent off 2,283 boxes to the unfortunate captives. The regulations of the Central Committee for Scotland had to be complied with as regards the number of articles in each box and the mode of addressing; inside was a post-card, with a number corresponding to the number of the parcel, and this card was sent home by the recipient of the box.

All this work necessitated an elaborate system of book-keeping. The ledger account contained full details of every article sent to each prisoner, and the stock book dealt with the stores which passed through the premises and which amounted to an annual value of over £50,000. Moreover, for each man a special file was kept in which all letters about him and from him were preserved and indexed. Periodically the premises were examined by Government Inspectors, whose reports contained unstinted praise for the manner in which the work was done at Royal Circus.

The voluntary workers never grudged time or labour in the service of the Regiment. For over two years the office work of the organisation was transacted by a number of ladies who attended daily from 9.30 a.m. to 6.30 p.m., while in the packing centre there were many retired workers who devoted the whole of their time to the cause, seeking no fee or reward except the gratification of working for fellow-countrymen, spinning out a dreary existence in prison camps.

And so it was all across the nation. But no organization can run smoothly without the efforts of key individuals, and in the POW welfare context there were many of these, most of them women, who rose to the demands of the task magnificently. The distribution of bread supplies to British POWs in Germany was organized by Lady Evelyn Grant Duff, a formidably efficient woman, who arranged for flour to be imported into Switzerland from Marseilles, and for the bread to be baked in Geneva, taken by road or rail to Frankfurt – where another Red Cross bureau had been set up – and from there sent to the various POW camps. Other bread supplies came from bakeries in Holland and Denmark. The bread reaching the camps through this organization, although hardly fresh, was scarcely ever more than a week old. Later in the war, a scheme was involved whereby camps were issued with bread in the winter and biscuits (rusks) in the summer, as summer heat turned bread mouldy very quickly. This, however, did not become effective until 1918; at the same time, the geographical lines for distribution were redrawn, with Berne assuming the responsibility for two-thirds of the camps in Germany and Copenhagen taking charge of one-third.

One aspect of prisoner-of-war welfare that gave serious concern from the beginning was the repatriation of sick or disabled men, and this hinged entirely on the independent inspection of POW camps and the state of the prisoners. The concern was inflamed, in the winter of 1914–15, by persistent reports that prisoners on both sides were being ill-treated. As the United States was looking after the diplomatic interests of both Britain and Germany, it was also suggested that she take care of POW interests, and in January 1915 an agreement was reached whereby the American Ambassador and his representatives should have the right to visit POW camps at twenty-four hours' notice. As a result of this, the first exchange of disabled British and German prisoners took place via Switzerland on 15 February 1915.

Repatriated French prisoners and British POWs from camps in central and southern Germany mostly went to Switzerland in the first instance, as did German prisoners who had been held in French camps. British POWs from the northern and eastern camps were repatriated via Holland, and German prisoners went that way too. Wherever possible, prisoners of equal rank were exchanged in similar numbers. Corporal John Brady of the King's Own Yorkshire Light Infantry, his health broken after three years and eight months of forced labour, imprisonment, and brutal treatment (although, in fairness to the Germans, it should be said that he had made repeated escape attempts and struck German civilian workers on several occasions), received a telegram, quite out of the blue, in April 1918 to say that he was to go to Aachen and then to Holland, to be exchanged for a German corporal.

Brady, who thought it was all a dream, 'kept very quiet till I crossed the border'; but it was true, and he reported in his long letter to his wife from an internment camp at The Hague that he was being treated exceptionally well and regaining his strength.

The idea was that repatriated POWs were to be given the best of treatment in the neutral camps, and be nursed back to full health before returning home. It was not always the case, however. All was not happy in the Swiss internment camps, as the following document reveals. Compiled in 1917, it is fairly lengthy, but deserves repeating here in full because it highlights the shortcomings of the repatriation system, which it must be remembered was still quite experimental. The report reads:

> On the whole the prisoners in Switzerland do a great deal of grumbling. They grumble at the work, six hours a day, they grumble at not being paid, they grumble at having to pay duty on things received from England, they grumble at the number of mothers allowed to visit Switzerland being restricted. The work

at Mürren is particularly complained of, as it consists of clearing snow, under the orders of British officers and NCOs. Some soldiers fear that soon they will be sending home for rifles to make them drill.

There are a good many complaints of the Swiss Commission. They say it does not even read men's papers nor inspect. The consequence of this is that many of the genuinely sick are left in Germany, and those only a little sick sent to Switzerland. The Commission is really a lottery.

Mürren

Canadian officers here sympathise with the men in their resentment at being ordered to do such heavy work. Classes for training men are in full swing at Mürren. Tailors' and carpenters' shops have already repaid the capital lent them, and are profit-earning businesses for the Red Cross. The educational classes have 170 candidates, who attend regularly. The men work for 1st, 2nd and 3rd class school certificates. The most successful of these experiments is the motor class, which has turned out 40 first-class chauffeur mechanics, and has 73 men waiting. Very good classes for first aid are arranged in French and German, and there are also small classes in Italian, Spanish and Russian. One man writing in February (1917) says 'We have an orchestra of 26 men, and have classes in shorthand and book-keeping.'

26.3.17. The hospitals are working at full pressure. Our men are assisted back to a semblance of their former selves. One of the greatest assets, from the soldiers' point of view, is a dental surgeon, a lecturer on dental surgery and histology at the University of Liverpool. He has been the greatest blessing to the interned, who suffer badly with decayed and aching teeth. I understand he is there entirely on his own initiative. He is a most amiable and kind man, and has endeared himself to all hearts.

If a man did work in Germany he got extra food for it. Here we get nothing at all. The German officer was civil to us, and treated us with respect. There was nothing in the way of a soldiers' room when we first got here. Then a certain Presbyterian minister, the Rev. Sutherland, started one, which was highly appreciated by the soldiers. When Lord Northcliffe came round he was carefully guided away from this room, and went back to England saying that we had no soldiers' room. The consequence of this was that some unfortunate rich gentleman was gulled into parting with £1,000 for the purpose of building one. When this was built the Rev. Sutherland was ordered by the colonel to close his place. Now the poor soldiers go to a place where they get a far inferior cup of tea.

There are complaints that the French are better billeted, work with the Swiss guards, and enjoy better privileges. An order has come out forbidding girls to walk out with British soldiers.

One man says he has lost 17½ lbs since he left Germany.

Mürren is built on a ledge. It takes five minutes to walk from one end of the place to the other. During seven months of the winter no roads are passable.

Chateau d'Oex

Chateau d'Oex is better than Mürren, but it is a miserable little saucer of a place, surrounded by hills, covered in slush at times, and thoroughly unsuitable for wounded men. Some of our men have been there for nearly a year, and no settled employment has been arranged for them. Experts from home have now come out with lordly schemes, involving the spending of some thousands of pounds. No scheme now seems to be looked at which does not involve vast expenditure, and no doubt magnificent results will be obtained in months to come, but in the meantime the discontent is increasing. How can anyone expect that six hundred-odd idle men will be contented and happy? Why should our men be poked away like criminals, and put in places where work is impossible? Here there is a factory where boxes and the boards that go inside rolls of cloth are made by the French, who are paid proper wages, and everything is sent to France. Something of the same sort could be arranged for our men, though it might be difficult.

We are blasting rock on the top of a mountain 3,000 ft above Chateau d'Oex, but we are not rushed. We come down on Saturday morning, and go back on Monday morning, and get our food for the week. Others were sent out to farms, but found the hours too long. Fifteen hours a day for 3 fr. seems excessive.

Soldanelle and Other Hospitals

Soldanelle. Hospital conditions good, subsequent treatment

71

shockingly bad. The medical staff consists of seven private soldiers, called orderlies, in charge of a sergeant in the 2nd Buffs who is equally ignorant. Practically no nursing. The food consists of preserved cabbage, macaroni and rice, and hard meat. The cook is generally drunk, and everything is very bady cooked. In March the management was taken from Delachaux' hands, and a new manager provided with a staff of six nurses.

At Rougement 'no nurses'. At Rosinière the hospital in the middle of March was 'an absolute disgrace, no nurses'.

There are complaints everywhere that nearly all the soldiers coming from Germany need operations and medical treatment, but no provision was made at first for these things in Switzerland.

The hospital at Soldanelle having been put on a satisfactory basis, the Rougement hospital in April called for attention. It was visited by Lord Edward Cecil and Colonel Picot, and it is to be feared that they may have been misled as to the real condition of affairs under the guidance of a prejudiced party.

There is also a hospital at Interlaken.

Lucerne

The English people are allowed out on Mondays, Wednesdays and Fridays from 2–5. There are also French, Belgians and Germans here. The Germans writing from here say that they are well treated, but most people think there are too many Germans here.

Leysin

The discipline here is very strict. A workshop forms part of the YMCA huts. The list of trades includes motor engineering, carpentry and wood-carving.

Geneva

There are three university students from Mürren here. 'It is a great thing to have escaped from the miserable restrictions and red tape of Mürren. Here you can do practically what you like so long as you are in by 9.30. There are 17 French prisoners attending courses. The rector of the University welcomed us warmly. "Gentlemen, you are at home," he said.'

Vevey

'Our men are very badly treated compared with the French. There are 20,000 French and 2,000 English. The French are in a charming spot, working at their usual vocations, walking about with girls, leading perfectly normal and seemingly contented lives. Our poor men are tucked away in the hills, treated as if they were all likely to become drunk at every possible moment, and made to feel as much prisoners as they were in Germany. Only about 200 of our men are genuinely employed in work which will be of the least use to them after the war.'

Gunten

One prisoner is 'delighted to get away from that miserable Mürren. We are making carpets for the British Red Cross, and have an enormous amount of orders for them. We can keep ourselves in cigarettes. It is very interesting work. We can put in our own hours of course, being piece work.'

Montreux

'It is perfectly scandalous the way our interned are neglected. There are many men here limbless and many officers too for whom nothing is being done, whilst the French are immediately looked after. If I had been in Germany I could have purchased a Boche leg. Nice thing for a neutral country to see our men going about on crutches without artificial limbs, and not one Frenchman. [This was in July 1917.]

Some of the German prisoners say they were well treated in England, and prefer the English camps to Swiss ones.

The writer says that Monsieur Quenod is to be put in charge of the Bureau de Secours in Berne, and that nothing but bread in future is to be sent from here, but as the bread from there is very bad, and most of the prisoners' bread is sent from Denmark, this is not of very great consequence. This arrangement was to begin on August 1st.

'I have had a row with the Bread Bureau. They have spent £14,000 on wages last year, and now Lady Grant Duff has left it in full control of a Swiss American, Bernsteil, so of course we cleared out.'

June 1917: 'There are now 1,800 British prisoners interned in

Switzerland, and 17,000 French. It is inexcusable, and is entirely the fault of the English. The Germans do not object to our men coming here, and we have not yet reached the limit of numbers agreed to by the Swiss Government. At Rosinière 30 men refused to go to work. They went on strike, and have been sent to prison, which is just what they want.'

July and August. Still dissatisfaction amongst the men on account of the amount of work they are expected to do for small wages, also on account of the selection of men for repatriation. Prisoners who reach Switzerland from Germany expect to find a land of plenty and a life of laziness. A good many of the men are marrying Swiss girls.

The warning about the poorness and scarcity of food, and the wretchedness of conditions in Switzerland is considered serious in anticipation of the coming winter. At Mürren 'the food is sour and the smell horrible'. At Piotta and Piora the men are wretchedly housed, having continually to move their beds on wet nights, and are overrun with rats. 'People in England think we have plenty of milk and cheese, for Switzerland is famous for it. From my balcony here I see loads of cheese for Germany.'

In September men write from Switzerland that they do not expect a large number of prisoners to come through from Germany, as a serious epidemic has broken out, and many men are dying. 'We hear it is typhus.' Men are dying at the rate of nine a day from typhus at Mannheim, it is said.

There are very serious complaints about the men who are repatriated from Switzerland. Some of the men who have never required any medical treatment in Switzerland at all are repatriated, whilst others with running wounds are being kept.

'Piotta is a dirty rotten old cow-shed.' (In the words of a prisoner.)

One man writes from Geneva: 'Plenty of work on the railway, 6 a.m. to 6 p.m.'

Another from Chateau d'Oex: 'Properly starved here, and miss Leysin very much.'

Lord Edward Cecil visited Switzerland at the beginning of April. Colonel Picot is not popular. There are a great many complaints of the behaviour of the English, who it is said make a point of being rude to the Swiss people, and encourage German waitresses and other girls. There is some talk of putting men on the land, but one man says: 'I am sure no man would do duty on the land for 2d an hour, unless he got extra food of course.'

The senior chaplain in Switzerland reported in April on the 'penitential settlement at Chateau d'Oex. Lord Edward saw this place and talked to this chaplain.'

It is suggested that the industrial centres for our prisoners in Switzerland should be Vevey, Meiringen and Seeburg, it being obviously unsuitable that mountain resorts should be used as centres of re-education. It is desirable that fit men, that is to say men who have become fit from residence in Switzerland, should be separated from invalids, so that an active and industrious spirit should be stimulated. After a couple of years in Germany many men become hopeless wasters, and have no inclination to do a hand's turn of any kind. If they are segregated from the invalids, they would not be distracted from applying their minds to learning a new craft by the presence of non-workers.

The Swiss practice of using repatriated POWs as cheap labour was not generally known at the time, and there would certainly have been a major outcry if it had been. The principal problem was that there was a very large pro-German element in Switzerland; this was understandable, as the German-speaking Swiss represented the largest slice of the population. The prime movers behind the Red Cross based in the country were almost all drawn from the French-speaking element, with a natural affinity towards the French. Nevertheless, it is too easy to be hard on the Swiss; their orderly lives must have been seriously perturbed by the influx of thousands of alien POWs, many of them sick and disabled. Moreover, the feelings of men who want to go home at the earliest opportunity after perhaps years in a POW cage, and who are prevented from doing so by quarantine regulations, are apt to run high.

1 Donington Hall, near Derby – the former ancestral home of the Hastings family – was used as a POW camp for German naval and military officers during the 1914–18 War. Kapitänleutnant Gunther Plüschow succeeded in escaping from here in July 1915 and stowed away on a ship bound for Holland.

2 Kapitän Maerker, the captain of *HIMS Gneisenau* – sunk during the Battle of the Falkland Islands in December 1914 – was an early inmate of Donington Hall.

3 German prisoners being escorted to an assembly area during the Battle of Flers-Courcelette, September 1916.

4 A captured German machine-gun crew pictured during the savage fighting around Arras, April 1917.

5 Civilian internees making their way to Ruhleben Camp in 1914. The men
appear cheerful enough, doubtless believing that it would 'all be over by
Christmas.' Four years of harsh reality lay ahead of them.

6 Prisoners queueing up for their rations at Ruhleben.

7 Scorning the poor facilities provided by the Germans, the internees in Ruhleben set up their own businesses and entertainments. Here, a group of internees looks forward to a performance at the 'Ruhleben Empire'.

8 A boxing match in progress at Ruhleben. Entertainments such as this played a vital part in sustaining morale, which remained generally good.

9 British, French and German walking wounded receiving treatment at a casualty clearing station during the Battle of the Lys, April 1918.

10–12 The British Officers' POW camp at Holzminden was notorious for its escape bids, mainly by tunnel. These three photographs (10, 11 and 12) show the big tunnel, seen here after excavation by the Germans, through which twenty-nine British prisoners escaped in July 1918. Ten reached neutral territory.

Tunnel
Entrance

Way in
to Tunnel
Entrance

11

12

13 Royal Marine Infantry pictured after their capture during the daring raid on Zeebrugge on St George's Day, 1918. Despite being prisoners, their bearing seems more disciplined than that of the German naval guard on the right.

14 German prisoners under guard in August 1918. The Ludendorff Offensives of the previous spring have failed, and Germany has already lost the war. To judge by their faces, these men know it.

15 British officers at Schweidnitz POW camp await repatriation after the Armistice. It was often a lengthy business.

16 British officer prisoners at Clausthal, in the Harz Mountains. This was one of the better camps, with good food and accommodation.

17 German prisoners surrendering on the Somme, May 1918.

REPRISALS AND IMPRISONMENT

Reprisals against prisoners of war, surprisingly, were not prohibited by the Land Warfare Regulations of 1907; in fact, it was to be 1929 before a set of rules prohibiting this kind of treatment was drawn up at Geneva. Given the fact that reprisals against POWs were therefore not considered illegal under international law, it is to the credit of all parties that such reprisals were not carried out on a larger scale.

In fact, reprisals for acts other than attempted escapes appear to have been initiated by the British, or more specifically by Winston Churchill, who was then First Lord of the Admiralty. Early in 1915, he ordered that captured German submariners were to be confined not in POW camps, but in the Naval Detention Barracks at Chatham and Devonport. As the Germans were not at that time waging unrestricted U-boat warfare, this action led to the German Admiralty feeling justified in retaliating by placing thirty-nine British officers in 'arrest barracks', which virtually meant that they were confined in cells in military prisons. The whole sorry business came to an end when Churchill was succeeded in the Admiralty post by Arthur Balfour in May 1915; one of Balfour's first announcements, made to the House of Commons on 9 June, was that his predecessor's policy had been abandoned and that from then on all U-boat prisoners would be treated as ordinary prisoners of war; this also applied to the survivors of shot-down zeppelins which had been raiding England (although such survivors were few), even though there was a considerable public demand for them to be treated as criminals.

There were other reprisal actions at intervals throughout the war. In 1917, when the Germans received word that the French were using German POWs to dig trenches in the front line – contrary to the stipulations of the Hague Rules – they made a large number of French prisoners do likewise. (In fact, the French and Germans had been using their respective prisoners for this purpose since the war began, although it is not clear who started the practice.) On a more minor scale, there were many other acts of reprisal; in the summer of 1917, for example, two RFC officers – Lieutenant G. S. M. Insall, VC, and Lieutenant G. C. Formilli – were imprisoned in tiny cells at Krefeld in retaliation for alleged ill-treatment of German officer POWs in Britain. As a consequence of frequent reports of such actions, a conference between representatives of the belligerents was arranged at The Hague in July 1917. It was agreed, among other points, that in no case should a belligerent resort to reprisals unless four weeks' notice of his intention had been given to the government whose personnel were affected.

One form of reprisal, which became more frequent as the war progressed and which in fact was more in the nature of an attempted deterrent, was to concentrate prisoners in areas which were subjected to enemy air attack. Some instances of this are recorded in *Air Power and War Rights* (London: J. M. Spaight, 1933), as follows:

> *The case of Karlsruhe.* During 1917 . . . Germany did take steps to use prisoners as hostages against air attack, though the date at which this policy was adopted is not clear. There was certainly an internment camp at Karlsruhe early in 1917, and it was reported unofficially that its establishment was the result of various raids upon the city, culminating in that of 9 January, 1917. It was installed, we are informed by a historian, near the royal residence and the railway station, in order that the danger to the French and English officers concerned might lead to a cessation of their compatriots' air attacks.
>
> An English officer (Lt Joseph Lee) who was interned there records the fact that the camp was in the centre of the town, surrounded by high buildings, hotels, restaurants, and mansions, but does not state whether its being so located was for the purpose of protecting the neighbouring buildings or not. He adds that the site had been the scene of a tragedy in the spring of 1916, when a large number of civilians, including women and children, were killed by bombs dropped by Allied airmen. The attacking airmen bombed, unintentionally, a crowd of people seeking

admission to the circus and menagerie which were at that time located in the square. Whether it was with the object of preventing further attacks that the *Kriegsgefangenenlager* was installed in this particular place one cannot tell. At any rate it was reported from Switzerland at the end of April, 1917, that large numbèrs of British officers were pouring into this camp, which, it was stated, had been established 'as a precaution against the bombardment of the town by Allied aviators'. It is, however, by no means certain that the camp at Karlsruhe was not an ordinary transit or concentration camp – a *Durchgangslager* – for prisoners of war. At any rate Mr Bonar Law informed Col. C. Lowther, in reply to a question in the House of Commons, on 21 June 1917, that: 'It has been formally stated by the German Government that the internment of Allied officers in the prisoners' camp at Karlsruhe has no connection with the policy of reprisals.'

The cases of Freiburg and Stuttgart. Freiburg-in-Breisgau and Stuttgart were other towns in which the policy of the *'paratonnerres'*, or lightning-conductors, as the French called it, was adopted. On 14 April, 1917, Freiburg had been the objective of a particularly damaging English raid, in reprisal for the submarine attacks on British hospital ships, and the University there, especially the medical school, had suffered very severely. A Berlin semi-official message of 12 May, 1917, stated that a new camp for prisoners of war had been established in the town, in a number of hotels, and that British and French officers of all ranks were being transferred thereto. In January, 1918, some 400 prisoners were in the town, distributed in various districts, and it is stated that nearly 50 had been killed by bombs dropped by Allied aircraft. Prisoners were also kept in various parts of Stuttgart, in order, said a German paper, that they might share with the population the dangers of air attack. (*Frankfurter Zeitung*, 31 December 1917.)

If there is evidence to show that the Germans deliberately set up POW camps in populated areas threatened by air attack, there is also plenty of evidence that they took steps to make sure that Allied airmen knew of their existence. While the surrounding area would be blacked-out, the camps were usually well lit. In fact, one French pilot held captive at Karlsruhe, Lieutenant Constantini, stated that the people of the town, believing that the raiding airmen knew the position of the camp and would carefully avoid bombing it, assembled round it as a sanctuary during the raids.

At the beginning of 1918, as *Air Power and War Rights* records, Great Britain adopted a similar policy.

As early as the beginning of February, 1916, a correspondent in the press had suggested that internment camps for prisoners of war should be formed near the more important munition factories. In May, 1917, the press agitation for the housing of prisoners in exposed towns was renewed, after the raid upon Folkestone towards the end of that month. [By this time, southern England was being attacked by formations of enemy bombers, mostly Gothas, which were causing heavy damage in some areas.] The Government refused to accept the suggestion that the Isle of Thanet should be safeguarded in this way. The agitation, however, continued, and the Government was driven to consider the matter. Mr Macpherson [the Under-Secretary of State for War] stated in the House of Commons on 22 January, 1918, that inquiries were still proceeding in regard to the truth of the allegations that our prisoners were being exposed to air attacks in Germany, and on 5 February, 1918, he informed the House that: 'Information has been received which leaves no doubt that the German authorities have placed officer prisoners of war in localities which are specially subject to air raids. Similar action is contemplated in this country.'

By May, 1918, a large number of German officers were established in requisitioned schools and other buildings at Ramsgate, Margate, and Southend. In one case at least the building in which the prisoners were housed had previously been used as a hospital for British or Dominion sick or wounded soldiers. Clearly, other things being equal, it was preferable on the grounds of humanity that able-bodied Germans should be exposed to air attack rather than our own disabled men, and if it had been a case of simple and inevitable exchange of quarters there would be little to be said. If, however, it was not a matter of exchange, direct or indirect, but of the removal from the south-east coast of the hospitals situated there to some fresh locality and the filling of the buildings thus evacuated with prisoners for whom there was plenty of accommodation in the camps in which they had hitherto been confined, the motive of the change was clearly not solely the humanitarian one of sparing our sick and wounded.'

Reprisals of the kind described above were one matter; imprisonment of POWs was quite another, and could be the result of a number of circumstances, the most frequent of which was attempted escape. Prisoners of war, as agreed by the Hague Rules, might be fired upon, and if necessary killed, during an attempt to escape, and if recaptured before they succeeded in rejoining their own forces or reaching neutral territory they might be subjected to disciplinary punishment, although they might not be punished for a prior successful escape if they were subsequently recaptured. The term 'disciplinary punishment' excluded the death sentence.

The sentence imposed on a recaptured POW could be with or without hard labour, and in this respect there were variations in the treatment meted out by the belligerents; whereas the French would generally favour a relatively short sentence, with hard labour, the British and Germans appear to have preferred lengthier sentences without hard labour, although there were some notable exceptions. In May 1917, the anonymous NCO of the 1st Hampshires, having tried unsuccessfully to escape from Holzminden, was given fourteen days' solitary confinement followed by a similar period of hard labour. He made another unsuccessful attempt in October, and was court-martialled at Harburg and sentenced to a month's hard labour in Cologne prison, working in the stone quarry. On his next attempt in December, which also failed, he received three months' hard labour at Cologne, and then he was sent to the POW camp at Harburg – which, in effect, was a punishment camp – where his troubles really started.

At Harburg . . . I was treated very badly by the sergeant and guard who were in charge of us; all extra clothing was taken away. Then fever got hold of me and I was ill for a week, but was not allowed treatment. On Sunday morning, owing to their behaviour to us, we all refused to work – Russians and the Frenchmen included, and when the guard used force against us a brawl started which developed into a free fight. I was put out very early on by a clout across the shoulder with a rifle, and we suffered considerable casualties, but so did our jolly hosts! The fight ended with reinforcements from the Company all fully armed. The French and Russians agreed to work half day on

Sunday, but we English were made to stand on tip-toe and trussed up all day to iron posts. If we wished to take the weight of our bodies off our feet we had to hang on to the ropes which bound us up. At 6 a.m. we were turned out of the hut, and at 7 a.m. we were neatly trussed up, with a basin of water two yards in front of us but no food or water till 9 p.m., a sentry standing by jeering at us. Later I was brought to a court-martial for leading a mutiny and was threatened with death. But this they dare not sentence me to, and I got two months' hard labour.

The test case for imposing the death sentence on a POW, in Germany at least, had come in January 1915, when a Private Lonsdale had been court-martialled and sentenced to death for striking a guard. The incident caused a diplomatic flurry and the sentence was commuted to twenty years' imprisonment, of which Lonsdale, naturally, served less than five.

Lonsdale had committed a serious offence under the military code of the country in which he was captive, and his punishment (although severe in the extreme) was justified. That imposed on another POW was not. In September 1917, Sergeant E. A. Boyd, who was attached to the Royal Naval Air Service, was flying as an observer in a seaplane when it was shot down by a German torpedo-boat off Ostend. Just before the ditched aircraft sank, Boyd scrawled 'Shot down at 6.42, Picked up by the Huns' on a message slip which he was just about to attach to the leg of a carrier pigeon when he and the paper were seized by the enemy. Boyd was tried before the military court, where it seemed that the principal charge was one of 'insulting the German defence forces', the insult being the single word 'Hun'. He was sentenced to a year's imprisonment. The British government protested at the absurdity of it, but to no avail; Boyd was still in goal when the Armistice came in November 1918.

ONES WHO GOT AWAY

For the Allied prisoners of war in Germany during 1914–18, the prospect of escape was a good deal more attractive – and practical – than was the case for another generation of POWs in 1939–45. For one thing, the whole of Western Europe was not occupied, and, while Switzerland remained the obvious target for prisoners in central and southern Germany, neutral Holland and Scandinavia beckoned to those in the northern camps. Escape from a work party, or from a train moving between prison camps, seemed to be the two best alternatives.

Major A. J. Evans, one of the 'bad boys' of Ingolstadt's Fort 9, decided that the time had come for him to make his getaway when it was announced that the more unruly inmates were to be transferred to Zorndorf in East Prussia. Together with another officer named Buckley, he decided to leap off the train at the first opportunity. This both men managed without injury, and apparently unnoticed by the guards. Then they set off to walk to the Swiss frontier, 200 miles away. It was 9 June 1917. As Evans recalled:

> We only walked by night and lay up in hiding through the hours of daylight – which was, I think, the worst part of the business and wore out our nerves and physical strength far more than the six or seven hours' marching at night, for the day seemed intolerably long from 4.30 a.m. to 9.30 p.m. – seventeen hours – the sun was very hot, and there was little shade, and we were consumed with impatience to get on. Moreover, we could never be free from anxiety at any moment of those seventeen hours. The strain at night of passing through a village where a few lights still burnt and dogs seemed to wake and bark at us in every house,

never worried me so much as a cart passing or men talking near our daytime hiding places.

We went into hiding at dawn or soon after, and when we'd taken off our boots and put on clean socks we would both drop asleep at once. It was a bit of a risk – perhaps one of us ought to have stayed awake, but we took it deliberately since we got great benefit from a sound sleep while we were still warm from walking. And it was only for about an hour before we woke again shivering, for the mornings were very cold and we were usually soaked with dew up to our waists. Then we had breakfast – the great moment of the day – and rations were pretty good at first, as we underestimated the time we would take by about four days. But later on we had to help things out with raw potatoes from the fields, which eventually became our mainstay. All day long we were pestered with stinging insects. Our hands and faces became swollen all over, and the bites on my feet came up in blisters which broke and left raw places when I put on my boots again.

On the fifteenth day our impatience got the better of us, and we started out before it was properly dark, and suddenly came upon a man in soldier's uniform scything grass at the side of the road. We were filthily dirty and unshaven and must have looked the most villainous tramps; it was stupid of us to have risked being seen, but it would have aroused his suspicion if we'd turned back, so we walked on past him. He looked up and said something we didn't catch. We answered 'Good evening' as usual. But he called after us, and then when we took no notice shouted 'Halt! Halt!' and ran after us with his scythe.

We were both too weak to run fast or far, and moreover we saw at that moment a man with a gun about fifty yards to our right. There was only one thing to be done, and we did it. We turned haughtily and waited for our pursuer, and when he was a few yards away Buckley demanded in a voice quivering with indignant German what the devil he meant by shouting at us. He almost dropped his scythe with astonishment, then turned round and went slowly back to his work. Buckley had saved the day.

The end of their march on the following night brought the two within about ten miles of the Swiss frontier, so they decided to eat the remainder of their food, with the exception of a few meat lozenges kept in case of an emergency, and cross over on the night after. They had memorized the details of their escape map so as to avoid having to strike matches later on, and left all their spare kit behind in order to travel light over what they hoped would be the last lap, but it was not to be quite as simple as they had anticipated.

We were awfully weak by now and made slow progress through the heavy going, and about two hours after we'd started a full bright moon rose which made us feel frightfully conspicuous. Moreover, we began to doubt our actual position, for a road we'd expected to find wasn't there. However, we tramped on by compass and reached a village which we hoped was a place named Riedheim, within half a mile of the frontier. But here we suddenly came on a single line railway which wasn't on our map. We were aghast – we were lost – and moreover Buckley was fearfully exhausted for want of food, so we decided to lie up for another night in a thick wood on a hill.

They ate the meat lozenges they had saved, and also managed to find water and some more raw potatoes. As soon as daylight came, they tried to establish their exact position. For all they knew, they might already be in Switzerland.

It was no good looking for signposts, since they'd all been removed within a radius of ten miles from the frontier. I think we were both slightly insane by now from hunger and fatigue; anyhow, I decided to take a great risk. I took off my tunic and walking down into the fields asked a girl who was making hay what the name of the village was. It was Riedheim – as I'd originally thought. The railway, of course, had been made after the map was printed. I don't know what the girl thought of my question and appearance; she gave me a sly look, but went on with her work.

I returned to Buckley, and when it was quite dark we left our hiding place. We had three-quarters of an hour to cross the frontier before the moon rose – and we had to go with the greatest care. For a time we walked bent double, and then we went down on our hands and knees, pushing our way through the thick long grass of water meadows. The night was so still – surely the swishing of the grass as we moved through it must be audible for hundreds of yards.

On and on we went – endlessly it seemed – making for a stream which we had seen from our hill and now knew must be the boundary line. Then the edge of the moon peered at us over the hills. We crawled at top speed now, until Buckley's hand on my heel suddenly brought me to a halt. About fifteen yards ahead was a sentry. He was walking along a footpath on the bank of a stream. *The* stream. He had no rifle, and had probably just been relieved. He passed without seeing us.

One last spurt and we were in the stream and up the other bank. 'Crawl,' said Buckley. 'Run,' said I, and we ran. It was just after midnight when we crossed into Switzerland and freedom on our eighteenth night out.

Another RFC officer who took his first steps to freedom from a train was Captain Champion. On learning that Vohrenbach was to be turned into a reprisal camp for French prisoners exclusively, and that all British and Russian officers were to be moved to Heidelberg, he decided to escape, together with his observer, Lieutenant Newbold, and two other officers, Lieutenants Ward and Mackay. It was April 1917 when they made their exit from the train at a small rail halt and began walking south. Eventually, after some minor adventures but no serious trouble, they came within sight of the Swiss frontier.

We climbed, stumbling and falling, for what seemed years. As we climbed, the snow, no longer in patches, handicapped us more and more. At last we reached some trees. We were absolutely lost. No stars were visible, we had no idea of direction and could not see more than the bare outline of trees near us against the snow. The cold was intense and we were wet to the skin. The only thing was to keep on the move, but in what direction? The frontier we knew must be near and probably guarded, perhaps barbed wire, perhaps electrified wire as on the Dutch frontier. If we stood still we should freeze to death.

The wind had been North East, and I thought that we might take the damp side of a tree to be the NE as the rain would beat against that side, but my hands were too cold to feel anything and it was too dark to see. We gave it up as hopeless and very cautiously made our way in the direction which we thought to be South. Through woods, down banks, up inclines, the ground seemed very broken. Once we came out of a wood into what seemed to be fields. We crept along a fence, when suddenly we saw somebody. We lay flat on the snow. . . . How long this terror lasted I don't know, but I suppose I got so cold I could stick it no longer. I got up and crawled forward. It was a plough!

. . . Dawn gave us our direction and we walked due South as fast as we could. On coming to a small hollow with very steep sides Ward found that he was not strong enough to climb the other side. Poor fellow, he was very distressed and his knee was giving him pain. [Ward had been wounded before capture.] In order to save his strength we decided to keep to the more level ground, which meant that we had to go east. Before long we came to a road, and seeing some houses further down, decided to investigate. On nearing the first house on the road we could discern the white cross on a red shield. The Swiss coat of arms and probably a post office. We were too worn out to show signs of elation, but silently shook hands. Switzerland at last.

In the north, one of the easiest places from which to escape was Ruhleben, the civilian internment camp. Here, a variety of escape options were open to the inmates, and they took full advantage of them. One of the leading escapers was A. E. Keith, a British businessman who had been living in Nuess, a town on the Rhine, when war broke out.

His first attempt was made from Dr Weiler's sanatorium on the outskirts of Berlin; according to his account, getting out of it was as easy as falling off a log.

I got up in the small hours of the morning, dressed, came downstairs in my socks, carrying my boots, opened a French window and issued forth, unseen and unheard by anyone, travelled by tram to Berlin and thence by train to Leipzig, where I bought a compass and some maps, and thence in other trains took a cross-country journey to the neighbourhood of the Dutch border.

Keith had the advantage of being a fluent German speaker. His account is revealing, showing as it does the laxity of German security precautions on their public transport system. There were no guards to check identity documents at regular intervals, as there would be in the war that followed. Nevertheless, Keith's first attempt ended in capture; he was spotted by a German border guard and arrested.

He was sentenced to a period in the Stadtvogtei, the prison in Berlin, from which he promptly escaped again with another Briton, Wallace Ellison. In his words, 'a means of picking a lock were procured, and a lock was picked, and, in the end, we had nothing to do but open the door when nobody was looking and walk out'.

Once more he succeeded in getting close to the Dutch frontier, but once more he was frustrated.

It was November. The weather was very trying. The cold and the exposure were more than Wallace Ellison could stand. The day came when he could hardly drag himself along. We had to knock at a farmhouse door and ask for help. We were given help, for which we paid, and were allowed to warm ourselves before a roaring fire. We even picked up some topographical information which seemed likely to be useful. But we had no chance of using it. Our appearance at the farmhouse had aroused suspicions. There had been talk. People were looking for us. A lieutenant caught us. His manner was friendly.

Keith went back to the Stadtvogtei and solitary confinement. As soon as it was over he made plans for a third escape attempt, and two other internees named Tynsdale and Kent promised to join him. While still in Stadtvogtei Keith succeeded, by bribery and corruption, in obtaining a much better map of the frontier area. It showed him a possible alternative escape route, but a dangerous one; he would have to cross a formidable expanse of swamp, twenty-five miles in length and up to seven in width, that bordered the River Ems. As the swamp was regarded as impassable except in very dry summer weather, it was not likely to be patrolled in the winter months by cavalry and dogs, as other border areas were.

Together with sixteen other prisoners, Keith was sent back to Ruhleben in August 1917 following the intervention of the Dutch Minister, who was now looking after the interests of British prisoners in Germany following America's entry into the war, and it was from there that the next escape attempt was made.

Getting out of the camp was not really very difficult. There were means of crawling under the barbed wire, used by man after man, and apparently well known to everybody there except the soldiers who were guarding us. So, on 16 September, we availed ourselves of those means, taking with us, as food for each man, a bar of chocolate, two small cabin biscuits with dripping, one oatmeal cake specially baked for us by a friend, two or three pieces of sugar and half a dozen raisins, together with a tin of Horlicks malted milk tablets and a small flask of brandy. Other food, of course, we expected to buy en route.

They travelled by train as far as the Ems, passing through Hanover, Bremen and Oldenburg to arrive at Coppenburg, where they found a convenient rowing boat and crossed the river. The next obstacle was the swamp.

It was bitterly cold. . . . The wind rose and the rain fell, and we soon woke with our teeth chattering. But we stuck it, making a kind of arbour with the oak saplings which gave us partial shelter through the rest of the night and the whole of the following day. Then, at half-past five, we ate our last meal, divided the malted milk tablets which we had kept for emergencies, cut staves which we thought likely to be useful, waited as patiently as we could for darkness, and at half-past eight started on our last lap.

It was difficult going, though we were, as yet, only on the fringe of the swamp. Two or three wide drainage ditches were crossed with the help of their sluice gates, and we jumped the smaller ones with the help of our staves. Then came marshy meadows and open patches of water where, for about an hour, we were always in water above our ankles, frequently much deeper, taking our zigzag way through the shallowest places.

Then we came to the swamp proper. It was as flat and as black at first as a congealed lake of asphalt, covered with an exceedingly short growth, like very tiny heather plants, or their densely intertwined roots, and very springy with the congealed bog underneath. No sentries, I felt sure, would be standing in that trackless waste. So we had time to take notice of our surroundings, which were very eerie – a black circle surrounding us, and some white patches ahead.

The sudden sound of rifle fire from some woods to the north firmed their resolve and they plunged into the swamp.

The ground was now very unstable all about us. I could feel slow waves rolling sluggishly under my feet, caused by our footsteps on the thin carpet of vegetable matter covering the morass. It was an area of slime on which we were walking, and these areas of slime increased in number, flowed together. I lost my balance, and nearly fell into a bog from which I probably could not have extricated myself, but Kent threw an arm round me and jerked me back.

The ground got worse and worse, and presently we found ourselves in the peat cuttings – great yawning holes and ditches, running mainly from north to south, black, with sometimes a star or two mirrored in the foul water a foot or so below the edge. The passage had to be made across bridges of standing peat, hardly ever more than two feet wide, which swayed as we shuffled over them. Kent fell, pretty much as I had done, but his staff fell across the gap into which he was slipping and he succeeded in scrambling out.

Some time later the going became firmer, and they gradually emerged from the swamp. Eventually they came to a cottage and knocked on the door. After a few minutes a man emerged and they told him that they were English prisoners of war.

He gripped our hands and shook them warmly and insisted on our returning with him to his cottage. . . . His wife, in picturesque undress, fired a volley of questions at her husband, clasped her hands, shook ours and then began lighting the kitchener. . . . Then the table was loaded with things to eat. We had fried veal, bread, butter, and plenty of milk and hot coffee – all this offered to us spontaneously in a farm labourer's cottage at half-past two in the morning; and after the meal was over, our host guided us to a village, where everybody asked us to breakfast, and thence were taken by the village policeman to a military station at Ter Appel. There we were given a wash, another good meal, and a bottle of port, and were questioned by a friendly sergeant, who apologized for his inability to offer us more luxurious accommodation.

The warmth of the welcome extended to Keith and his friends was quite typical of the Dutch. Another escaper who experienced it was Private James McDaid of the 10th Battalion of the Argyll and Sutherland Highlanders, who had been captured at the Battle of Loos in September 1915. The summer of 1917 found him in Münster POW camp, where he teamed up with a Private Anderson ('Johnnie') of the Black Watch and Private Nielson ('Aggie') of the 8th Canadian Infantry. Nielson was of Scandinavian extraction and spoke fluent German. The three were working in the cavalry barracks at Münster, where civilians were also employed, and from there they decided to try for the Dutch border. Their civilian disguise, as McDaid explains, was rudimentary.

I managed to procure a sleeve waistcoat from a newly-arrived prisoner, and a soft hat that had been stolen from a scarecrow. We had a home-made map and a compass which I got from a Captain of the Gordons who was brought to our camp after an unsuccessful attempt to escape.

At this time we made the acquaintance of a German sentry who, for a couple of cakes of soap, a commodity the Germans had to do without during the war, told us of a road running parallel to the frontier and a few kilometres from it which was patrolled night and day by foot and cycle patrols. Consequently, the sentries on the frontier at this part were 400 yards apart instead of 200 yards as in other parts.

The first thing was to lull the German guards at the barracks into a sense of false security.

I noticed that the Germans kept a few pet rabbits, and also that there were a few dandelions in the compound. Before long I had gathered all the dandelions and given them to the rabbits. The Germans seemed quite pleased at this, so before very long I was outside the compound and round the side for a minute, returning with dandelions. The next time I was away for two minutes and so on until the Germans paid no attention if I was outside or round at the back, for I was only gathering dandelions for the rabbits. I noticed when round at the back that I was not conspicuously under the view of the sentry on the gate, and, with ordinary care, could avoid being seen by him. We decided to make the attempt on Thursday.

This was 16 July 1917, and there was an unexpected bonus. News had just reached the camp that the Kaiser had dismissed his Chancellor, von Bethmann-Hollweg; the guards were preoccupied with discussing the event and their attention was more relaxed than ever.

At mid-day the civilians engaged in the barracks began to leave. The first three of our guards had gone for macaroni. I had gone round to the back to gather dandelions. The other Germans had gone to join the macaroni queue. Johnnie and Nielson crept through the fanlight into the tool-shed and changed. I gave them the all-clear signal and they both came out. As they came out, I went in, changed, stuck the butt end of a cigar into my mouth, opened my paper and walked out.

Getting away from the camp was reasonably painless. The trio hid in a cornfield and then struck out across country after dark. On the sixth night they struck a road running north–south, but not the one that was their objective.

We lay a short distance off the road until we saw a patrol passing. As soon as they had passed, we crawled across the road on all fours. It was now a case of crawling all the time with a short twig in either hand in order to discover if there were any low-set live wires. Progress in this way was very slow indeed. We could now see the tracks where the sentries marched to and from their post on the frontier when being relieved. We came across a can of milk and drank most of it. It was the sentries' milk, so if we got caught now, we knew what to expect.

Shortly after this we came to a long stretch of wood through which we crawled very carefully. The cracking of twigs sounded to us like an artillery bombardment. . . . Suddenly we came to a clear cutting running through the wood as far as we could see on either side. Could this be the frontier? There were no sentries within our view. We crawled one at a time across this space wondering if we were in Holland when we got across. . . . There was a faint sign of daylight in the distance so we got into a cornfield to await nightfall again. We could hear voices all day but could not decide whether they were Dutch or German.

On the following night the escapers struck another road running north–south and decided to travel along it. According to their map, it ought to lead to the Dutch village of Winterswijk.

Several times we had to take cover in a ditch running alongside the road. On turning a bend in the road we suddenly came face to face with a sentry standing on the opposite side of the road. We expected to be challenged, but he never said a word. 'Speak to him, Aggie,' said Johnnie. 'If he's German, knock him out. We'll grab his rifle and run for it.'

Aggie bade him good morning in German. He replied in German and did not seem particularly interested in us. 'Are you Dutch?' asked Aggie. 'Yes,' replied the sentry. 'And you', he said, looking at us curiously, 'look like escaped prisoners.' (We had not been washed or shaved· for eight days and our clothes were in tatters.) 'We are,' said Nielson.

He explained that they were not Russians or French, but Englishmen – which was not strictly true.

At that, he threw down his rifle, threw his arms round our necks and hugged us. He called on the remainder of the guard to come out and meet three Englishmen (two of us were Scots and one a Canadian) who had run away from the Kaiser. That day the Mayor and his councillors came and welcomed us to Holland. In three weeks' time Johnnie and I were back in Bonnie Scotland and Nielson had gone home to Canada.

Escapers who were unfortunate enough to be recaptured some-times found, to their surprise, that their captors were sympathetic. Lieutenant Cecil Blain of the RFC escaped from Clausthal and got very close to the Dutch border before being arrested by a police sergeant. He said later:

This sergeant turned out to be one of the finest men I met in Germany – a thorough gentleman. He apologised for everything and was quite sorry for my ill luck. He told me everything, and it appears that I was about one kilometre off the frontier, had I gone along the road – but that the frontier was two hundred metres to my left and running parallel with the road at that place.

He took me into the town where I had a shave and a shampoo, and later a wash in my cell. All my meals came from the hotel, and I had them on parole with this sergeant and his wife in their sitting room. I only spent one day there, but the food was quite the best I had had since I landed on Hun soil.

Blain had quite a different reception when he returned to Clausthal, where the commandant was one of the infamous Niemeyer twins.

He shrieked and bellowed at everyone, posted two sentries outside each window and four on the door, while about three NCOs and two men surrounded me – the men with fixed bayonets. The men might have been rehearsing the scene by the way they stood in a semi-circle around me until Herr Hauptmann Niemeyer walked up and proceeded to tear the clothes off my person. I managed to palm my compass and twenty marks in real money – then after running their fingers through all the remaining seams of my clothes, I was escorted down in state to a new cell, in which I was locked with a sentry and fixed bayonet.

Blain was sent from Clausthal to Ströhen, but after a short time there went to Holzminden, which was run by the other Niemeyer twin; this one was nicknamed 'Milwaukee Bill' because he had been educated in the United States and spoke English with a nasal American accent. Like his brother, he modelled himself on the Kaiser, even down to the waxed moustache with upturned ends.

Blain promptly became involved in the major escape project at Holzminden, a tunnel which was the brainchild of a Canadian officer named Major Colquhoun. The entrance, only eighteen inches in diameter, was beneath a staircase. As Blain states,

> It was run on old-fashioned lines – no patent gadgets were used at all. We dug with table knives where there was soil, and progged about with a cold chisel and bits of rake through the stone. The soil and stone collected was drawn back in a basin on to each side of which a rope was attached so as it could be pulled backwards and forwards.
>
> This was one of the biggest tunnels that I had worked in. It was some sixty yards long, and was about as wide as the average fireplace, being roughly rectangular in shape also. The soil and rubble were disposed of by filling mattress covers stolen from our quarters, and these were stored under the staircase to the orderlies' quarters. By the time digging was finished the chamber under the stairs was packed to the limit with these 'sacks' of soil and rubble.
>
> Running about eight to nine feet below the ground surface, the tunnel twisted somewhat tortuously. There were several reasons for this. One was the difficulty in measuring direction accurately – our compasses were not so finely accurate for such purposes – and another was the difficulty of penetrating the stones which had apparently once formed a river bed. At one point we decided to descend another four feet or so in an attempt to get under this

stony strata, but finding this to be futile we decided to return to our previous level.

Toward the end the tunnel was so winding and hump-backed that it was no longer possible to use our rope and basin method of disposing of the rubble, so we had to resort to filling the sacks where we were working and dragging them back through the tunnel. This was a very wearisome task, particularly in the confined space available, for one had to wriggle backwards for a yard or so and then drag the heavy sack after him. However, this gave us some good practice for the night of the break-out, for then each man had to crawl forward on his elbows, pushing his pack in front of him – which was even more difficult!

The main illumination of the tunnel was candlelight, and a very creditable device was constructed for ventilating it. This device consisted of an ingenious set of bellows, hand operated, and constructed from the leather of an old RFC flying jacket, while the ventilating 'shaft' was made from biscuit tins, first having the bottom taken out, and then being joined together. We used wooden bed-boards stolen from our beds to revett the tunnel, and it was very wonderful that nobody's bed ever collapsed! There were many rats living in the tunnel, and meeting one of them and seeing the glitter of beady eyes in the semi-darkness was a feeling of revulsion only surpassed when one of the vile and foul creatures scurried over you.

The overall plan was that the tunnel – which in fact took nine months to construct – should be completed by the summer of 1918, emerging in the field of rye about fifty yards beyond the camp perimeter. The tall corn would provide adequate cover for the escapers. In the event, restrictions imposed upon the prisoners as a reprisal for the alleged ill-treatment of German POWs in Britain slowed down the work on the tunnel – there were, for example, four *Appelle* a day instead of two – and so the decision was taken to terminate it in a bean field short of the corn. To check on progress, as the tunnel began to angle upwards, a stick with a rag on the end was cautiously poked through the surface and its position noted by observers on top of one of the barrack blocks.

Thirteen men had been involved in the tunnel working party, and they were given priority in the escape attempt. A list of eighty-six other names was submitted, but selection was not easy. Parties had to be organized, and so had the escape route each party would take. The escape meetings seemed interminable, and, as Blain records:

> more arguments ensued as to the capabilities of various people and the places they should have. Nevertheless it was all settled finally, and on one wet night – 23/24 July 1918 – the tunnel was opened, and figures with big bags streamed out as in one huge crocodile, heads and feet all touching, to crawl behind beans, peas, and through high-standing corn, to break away each party for itself, and in its own special direction. . . . Twenty-nine got away that night, and one thing I regret is that I was not in the camp the next day to see Herr Hauptmann Niemeyer's face when the roll was called – I expect it was a wonderful show!

The reason that only twenty-nine prisoners managed to escape was that part of the tunnel collapsed at a critical moment, and some men narrowly escaped being buried alive. Nevertheless, of the twenty-nine who did get clear, ten successfully reached Dutch territory – and Cecil Blain was one of them. As he had surmised, 'Milwaukee Bill' was not at all happy. According to one officer who stayed behind, the commandant

> went off his head. He got *very* het up. I don't blame him really, because he was standing beside the barracks, and shouting. He had two sentries with him, when somebody on the top floor threw a great log out of the window at him. This infuriated him even more. He sent one of the sentries inside – to go and shoot somebody. I happened to be going innocently upstairs, and this man came and fired off his rifle just behind me. He wasn't trying to hit me – the bullet went out of the window. He just had to make a noise, but it frightened me to death. I came down quickly, and went back to my room.

Cecil Blain, when he was recaptured close to the Dutch border on his earlier escape attempt, mentions that he gave his parole to the German police sergeant. Strictly speaking, British officers and men who were taken prisoners in the 1914–18 war were not permitted to give their parole. A suggestion that they should be allowed to do so was made in the House of Commons on 10 July 1916, but Mr Asquith stated that he did not consider the proposal a practicable one. In a few exceptional cases, however, parole given by civilian internees was recognized. One such case involved a civilian named

Hollander, who was released from internment at Karlsbad (now Karlovy Vary, Czechoslovakia) on 24 August 1914 on giving his parole not to bear arms against the Central Powers. When the question of his being called up arose under the Military Service Act in March 1916, his parole was recognized and he was exempted.

The French and Germans both took the question of parole very seriously – so much so that, when a French pilot named Gilbert escaped from internment in Switzerland under circumstances which were held to amount to breach of parole, the French authorities sent him back again. Similarly, the Germans sent back to Holland two officers who broke their parole and escaped from internment.

Cecil Blain's reason for giving parole was impeccable; he had no wish to get the kindly police sergeant and his wife into trouble. For an officer – British, French, or Russian – to give parole while in prison camp, however, was in most cases unthinkable.

In fairness, it must be said that there were some POW camps from which very few escape attempts were made, and in a few cases none at all. The most attempts were made from the *Strafelager* (punishment camps) such as Ingolstadt, Holzminden, and Ströhen. The latter was literally riddled with tunnels, and held the record for the biggest number of successful escapes. Blain, who spent a fortnight there, reported that

> people just disappeared. . . . I wandered around as soon as I arrived and was rather surprised to see others doing the same thing just behind me. I tried to get away from them but could not, the real truth being that here were queues for escaping.

At Neuenkirchen, the prisoners had organized a veritable escape factory in a small room at the top of the house (which had originally been a Roman Catholic club). All sorts of escape kit were manufactured there; the snag was that the work involved a certain amount of hammering, which naturally attracted the attention of the Germans. As a cover, the prisoners constructed a Wimshurst machine, which was a device for generating static electricity. Using two contra-rotating discs, it produced a very loud rhythmical cracking noise when shorting to earth – a sound not unlike the tapping of a light hammer. The Germans might have wondered why the British should want to amuse themselves with such an odd toy, but they never questioned it.

The escape problem at Ströhen became so serious that on several occasions detectives were called in from Berlin to try and uncover the principal officers responsible. They failed, and on leaving the camp sometimes found that their pockets had been picked and their identity cards stolen. One was even seen to pass through the gate with a piece of paper bearing the words 'You know my methods, Watson!' pinned to his coat tail.

The fact was that the Germans were completely baffled by the sheer ingenuity – and sometimes downright cheek – of the British escapers, and of course the word 'British' includes men from the Dominions as well. The Germans were predictable in their methods, whereas the British were not. Yet the French and Russians could be equally enterprising. It was two French airmen, Commandant Menard and Lieutenant Pinsard, who held the record for covering the distance from Ingolstadt to the Swiss frontier – 240 miles in sixteen days. (Major Evans and Lieutenant Buckley, RFC, took eighteen days). Four more French airmen, De Tascher, Papeil, Amiot, and Chemet, escaped from the POW camp at Dillingen and followed an escape route that involved swimming the Rhine; three of them surmounted this dangerous obstacle, but Chemet was drowned.

Another remarkable escape involved an American officer, Lieutenant P. O'Brien, who was serving with the Royal Flying Corps. Shot down and captured in August 1917, he jumped off a train at Strasburg on 9 September and, instead of heading for Switzerland – which was much closer – he struck northwards towards Holland, exchanging his uniform piece by piece for stolen civilian clothing as he went. After a series of extraordinary adventures, passing as a Belgian worker and devoid of any means of identification, he reached Holland on 19 November after a journey of seventy-two days.

Perhaps the most enterprising escape attempt of all, however, involved a Russian colonel at Zorndorf, a camp not far from the eastern front. He made himself a German cavalry officer's uniform, manufactured a saddle and bridle from pieces of cardboard, and walked through the main gate intent on finding a horse on which he could make his escape to friendly territory. But no horse could be found, and after a while the sight of a rather bedraggled and horseless cavalry officer, carrying a saddle, inevitably attracted attention. It was not long before he was back in Zorndorf, and solitary confinement.

One of the last escapes from German captivity was made by an American naval officer, Lieutenant (Junior Grade) Victor G. Isaacs, who was serving on the 19,000-ton troop-ship *President Lincoln* when she was torpedoed 600 miles west of Brest by the U-90 on 31 May 1918. The vessel was *en route* to the United States with 715 persons on board, many of them sick and wounded. She was not a hospital ship and was therefore considered a legitimate target by the submarine's commander, Kapitänleutnant Joachim Remy.

Isaacs was picked up by the U-boat and, after a period in various transit camps, was put on a train bound for a permanent camp at Villingen, where the inmates were mostly Russian officers. Having made two or three unsuccessful escapes previously, he was determined to succeed this time. As he wrote later:

The train was making about forty miles an hour, and we were passing through a valley which was rather thickly populated. The guns of the guards were pointed toward me and they did look ugly; but the window near our seat was open and I was sure that I could reach it at a bound, so if they fired they would be just as likely to hit one of the other passengers as me. It was warm and close in the carriage and one of the guards was dozing. I waited until the other slightly turned his head to answer a question put by one of the soldiers with whom he was talking. Then, jumping up, with my knapsack hanging from my neck, I leaped past both guards and tried to dive through the window. It was small, probably eighteen inches wide and twenty-four inches high; and as there was nothing on the outside of the car to hold to, I had to depend on my momentum and the weight of my head and shoulders to carry the rest of my body along. My head and shoulders went through nicely; and then with the shouts of the guards ringing in my ears I simply fell and all went dark.

When I disappeared from view the guards must have pulled the bell-rope, for the train came to a stop about three hundred yards farther along. In the meantime I had landed on the track that paralleled the one on which the train was running. The bed was of crushed rock and the ties of steel. My head struck one tie and I was stunned, but rolled over and over; and the shaking up must have brought me again to my senses, for by the time the train had stopped I was struggling to my feet.

Then I made a terrible discovery: my knees had apparently

struck the tie next to the one that damaged my head, and when I tried to run I found they were so cut and bruised that I could not bend them. My feet, too, had been cut across the insteps, my body was all bruised and my hands and arms had small pieces of rock ground in; but in spite of all this no bones were broken. Had it not been for the condition of my knees I should have been able to make my escape; but by the time I was on my feet trying to shuffle away, the guards had descended from the train and were rapidly advancing toward me firing as they came.

I tried to run, but could make very little headway, and soon I was exhausted. My breath came in gasps and I finally fell to the ground. I was dragging myself along by pulling on the grass when the last shot passed between my ear and shoulder and buried itself in the ground in front of me. The guards were less than seventy-five yards away, and I just had time to turn over, raise myself to a half-sitting and half-lying posture and elevate my hands above my head as a sign that I surrendered, before they were on me.

With fiendish fury the first guard, turning his gun end for end and grasping it by the muzzle, rushed on me, and dealt me a smashing blow on the head. It knocked me unconscious and I rolled down the hill. When I came to my senses I was lying in a shallow ditch at the foot of the hill and the guards were cursing and kicking me trying to make me get up.

Many of the people from the hayfields nearby had gathered to watch the fun. Among them I noticed many women and children and a few old men. One old veteran with a pitchfork in his hands came running up and offered his services to the guards in case I should become dangerous. No-one in all that crowd offered a word of sympathy or tried to remonstrate with my captors in the punishment they were administering – and these were the best people of Germany, the pious, church-going Baden peasants!

And I must have made such a pitiable-looking spectacle! The blood was streaming down my face from the wound in my head where it had struck the railroad tie; my trousers at the knees had been ground into the flesh; and my hands were torn and bleeding. When they recaptured me they struck me on the head and body with their guns until one broke his rifle. It snapped in two at the small of the stock as he struck me with the butt on the back of the head.

Isaacs received two weeks' solitary confinement for this escape attempt, but there was no thought in his mind of giving up. While on board the U-90, he had learned many details of the submarine's internal workings, and the operational tactics employed, which he considered would be extremely valuable to the Allies. In fact, he considered the information in his possession to be so important that he had tried to jump off the U-90 when the boat was off the Danish coast, but had been seized by the crew and bundled below.

His next chance to escape, however, did not come until the night of 6 October, when, assisted by a number of US Army officers, he managed to short-circuit all the lighting circuits in Villingen POW camp and then cut through the barbed wire perimeter fences.

Sentries cried out 'Halt! Halt!' several times in rapid succession to me and my companion, an American officer in the French Army.

When we dropped to the ground we whirled and ran away from the camp and past the guards who had approached to within a few feet of the bridge. As we did so, both guards fired and the one on my right had the end of his rifle so close to my head that the flash seemed to singe my hair. But neither of us was hit during the next few minutes. There was a regular hail of bullets sprinkling the side of the hill. But as we were mere shadows only a little blacker than the darkness and moving swiftly we soon were completely blended with the surrounding obscurity.

I made my way for seven days and nights over the mountains to the Rhine, which to the south of Baden forms the boundary between Germany and Switzerland. After a four-hour crawl on hands and knees I was able to elude the sentries along the Rhine. Plunging in, I made for the Swiss shore. After being carried for several miles down the stream, being frequently submerged by the rapid current, I finally reached the opposite shore and gave myself up to the Swiss gendarmes, who turned me over to the American legation at Berne. From there I made my way to Paris and then London and finally Washington, where I arrived four weeks after my escape from Germany.

Isaacs sailed to the United States on the fast Cunard liner, now a troop-ship, the SS *Olympic*. He was later to receive the Congressional Medal of Honor for his exploits.

By coincidence, he arrived in Washington early on 11 November, and was standing in a window of the State, War, and Navy building alongside Assistant Navy Secretary Franklin D. Roosevelt some hours later, watching the crowds cheering President Woodrow Wilson across the street at the White House. The Armistice was official, and suddenly the Allies no longer had need of the information Isaacs had risked his life to bring home.

Chapter 8

THE CAMPS, 1918:
THE FINAL MONTHS

The massive haul of Allied prisoners, most of them British, that resulted from the German offensives of March–May 1918 had a twofold effect; for the first time in eighteen months the morale of the German civilian population, and that of troops in the rear areas – including those guarding the POW camps – reached a fresh peak, while the morale of the prisoners themselves plummeted to a new low. This was witnessed at first hand over a period of time by Trooper Walter Jowsey of the Royal Horse Artillery, who, having been captured in March, arrived with 1,200 other prisoners at Dülmen sanitation and distribution camp. All the local German civilians turned out to watch the prisoners' arrival, singing 'Deutschland über Alles'.

After a period of quarantine, the newly arrived prisoners were moved into Dümen's No. 2 camp, where there were numbers of Russians, Belgians, and Portuguese. After several weeks on what amounted to a starvation diet, British feelings ran high against the Russians, who according to Jowsey

> had absolutely hordes of grub, sent by the people of England while British prisoners were starving. They would not give us food, but would exchange it for watches, rings or anything of value. I sold a good ring for a few biscuits.

The British prisoners were set to work cleaning out the latrines. 'It was a rotten job. They always picked the English if there was a rotten job to do. German guards who could speak English said they had captured St Omer and 5,000 prisoners.'

Jowsey and some of his companions were sent to Friedrichsfeld in the Rhineland, where they were set to work in the local coal mines.

The camp also contained 250 French and 300 Russian prisoners, as well as 250 British and a similar number of other nationalities. It was now the last week in April; in Flanders the Germans were still on the offensive, and their successes were reflected by the arrogant attitude of some of the German civilians in the mine. Jowsey recorded in his diary that:

On the 27th we had to do a double shift . . . from 2 p.m. to 6 a.m., without coming to the top. It was on this shift that I got my first real impression of a German. When we were on a double shift the prisoners were allowed to go to the bottom of the shaft at 9.40 p.m. for soup. On this night I and a South African, and another chap, Private Kingston, asked the under-foreman if we could go and he said yes. On our way we met the head foreman, or *Steiger*; he asked where we were going and we told him. He said we were early, and without further warning he picked up a big metre stick and started to chase us. We all had our lamps and could see where we were going, but Kingston's lamp went out. He was last man. He tried to run on but caught his head with awful force on an iron roller suspended from the roof. This knocked him practically unconscious, and while he lay there the Steiger kicked him and struck him all over the head and body. We could not interfere as a party of Germans had gathered and were in sympathy with the Steiger.

We took Kingston to a shaft and after a lot of arguing we got him sent up. Even then they wanted him to work. The next day the poor chap tried to cut his throat. He was half mad with the pain in his throat. They fetched the camp commandant and the medical orderly, but they refused to do anything for him, saying that if he wanted to take his life he could, and hoped some of us would do the same. They grinned in his face and spat at him, and then left him. We did our best for him, and then the commandant said he would have to go to work, as he had done the injury himself. Considering the man couldn't stand up by himself it seemed ridiculous, but the German meant what he said. The interpreter got him off work after a lot of arguing. . . . They left him lying for another three days without attendance and then took him to hospital, where he died the same day. He was practically murdered, as he died from the wounds in his head. They buried him in a plain coffin, little better than a box, and took it on a cart. They said that was the way they buried people who tried to take their own lives in Germany.

The weeks passed, and in June the Germans were still convinced that their offensive was succeeding and that they were going to win the war.

The Germans keep telling us how they are advancing, and what they will do when they get to England. Some of the Germans down in the mine were pretty decent, but some were absolutely rotten. They would try to do you an injury all they could, try to drop coal or stone on your fingers or trap you between trucks. We also had to watch them pretty carefully; one chap, a lance corporal, died in hospital from a knocking-about he got from two Germans; they made his life absolutely hell on earth.

Kids about our own size used to throw coal and stones at us, but we laid in and gave them a good hiding, so they soon stopped that.

Another prisoner who found himself in the rough and sometimes brutal environment of a German coal mine was Able Seaman James Byrne, who early in 1918 was sent to a mine

near the Bohemian frontier, miles from any towns. We lived in a small wooden shed, just large enough to hold us all when we were in bed; the beds as usual were loose straw and no pillows and one blanket, it was bitterly cold and the snow was on the ground.

We were turned out next morning and taken out to our jobs. They gave me a shovel about two feet square and ordered me to fill fifteen tubs a day, and then I could pack up. Well this was impossible and I was kept there until I had finished them, that was from 6 a.m. till 10 p.m.; I was done in. However they gave me a lighter job as I was the smallest there, and the job was pushing tubs on to an overhead wire that took them to a factory about two miles away. Now the other fellows suggested that I should cause the wires to break over the field by putting the tubs on too close to each other; I thought that it was a good idea, so the week that I was on nights I put three tubs on close to each other and waited. I didn't have to wait long; there was a crash, and I knew what had happened. The civilians were going mad, and began punching and pushing me about all over the place. I tried to convince them that it was not my fault, but they knew

105

otherwise. The mine was out of action for 24 hours and all my pals clapped me on the back.

About 200 yards away there was another mine with other POWs working there, and we heard about one of them getting shot dead because he hit a civilian who was bullying him, although we didn't care what they did, we were so depressed and miserable. The beds were overcrowded with lice, and if we had not been so tired we could never have slept.

One day I put my finger on the line for the truck to smash it. God must have been with me because the truck wheel just pushed my finger away, and because I was being watched I did not try again. The next day I poured some boiling water over my hand. . . . I got four days rest, which I often think saved my life, because I felt myself going very low.

By the middle of 1918, there were enormous differences in the quality of the rations being issued to prisoners of war, and nowhere was the quality more variable than in the case of the POWs attached to working parties behind the front. Extracts from the diary of Private Reginald Bellamy for August 1918 read:

August 1. Work. Easy. Had half of French loaf and lard, also meal issue and made porridge for supper. Very good sour cabbage dinner. . . . August 4. Easy day. Another fine barley dinner with carrots. One-quarter loaf and cheese and gherkins for breakfast and one-quarter loaf for tea. . . . August 6. Very good barley meal and carrot dinner and one-third French loaf and lard tonight. . . . August 7. Work. One-quarter loaf for breakfast and very good barley and fruit dinner.

The anonymous diarist captured at Le Cornet Malo in April 1918, by way of contrast, was having a correspondingly hard time in June, sawing wood at Carvin.

June 27. Been here nearly two weeks and dislike it more every day. We are fetched out at 5.0 a.m. and one swine (a Prussian) delights in using his bayonet for the purpose. Sawing wood until 6.30 a.m. when we are given a kind of tea. At 7.0 a.m. we start for the Fabrik [factory] which is on the other side of Mortagne. We pass over the River Scheldt and a canal to get to it. It was evidently a large workshop of some sort, but all the machines had been removed. Our job has been to shift sand from the barges to the railway trucks. One man throws it from the barge to another man who throws it about three yards to the next man, and so on until it reaches the trucks. The treadmill would be a pastime to it, almost. It's not the hard work so much as the deadly monotony of the job. One of the guards (another Prussian) has an Alsatian dog which he sets at those he thinks are not working fast enough. I've seen a number of men suddenly bowled over by the dog with it standing over them with bared teeth at their throat. Beyond a scratch I don't think the dog bit them, but the effect on the men so treated can be imagined. The Prussian thought it a huge joke and would double up with laughter before he called the dog off. We go back to the fort at 1 o'clock for soup (boiled cabbage) and return to the Fabrik about 2 o'clock. We finish at 5.30 p.m. when we get a piece of bread and more tea. At 6.30 p.m. we are locked up for the night.

June 30 (Sunday). This is a worse day than the others. Today we have been to the Fabrik and this afternoon we were supposed to wash our shirts. Two tubs of water were given us and in these 100 shirts had to be washed. We have only one shirt each and as there was no means of drying them, I'm afraid many were put on wet after the washing. I managed to wet only the sleeves of mine without the guard noticing that the remainder of it was dry. How could 50 men wash filthy shirts in a tub of cold water without soap? Everyone was ordered to have his hair cut close with clippers and Jerry would of course choose to shout 'fall in' when only half of mine was cut. Our beds, which are made of plaited straw, are alive with lice, and I have slept on a form about eight inches wide for some nights now.

July 7. Still working at wood shifting. Saw a Jerry hit an Italian with the butt of his rifle this morning and he has an eye like a prize-fighter. On our way back to the fort our planes bombed the town and we had to run. The civvies had a communion or something on, because all the girls were going to church dressed in white. One bomb fell just outside the church but fortunately nobody was hit. Taken to the river this afternoon for a bathe. The mud at the bottom was over our knees so the only thing to do was swim about. Some couldn't swim and they clung to the bank to prevent themselves sinking in the mud. Before we had been there five minutes, the swine with the Alsatian came along and set the dog at those who had been holding on to the bank.

The lot of Corporal Arthur Speight of the 7th Durham Light Infantry, who, it will be recalled, had been repairing railways at Ramecourt and Amifontaine, had improved a little – but not much – by August 1918. Speight had now been moved to the village of Cilly and was engaged in clerical work. He records that the accommodation at Cilly was much better than at Ramecourt; the men were housed in barns fitted with wire bunks. They were also issued with clean shirts and underclothing. Dysentery, however, was still a scourge, and now many men were suffering from badly swollen and fluid-filled legs – a form of beriberi caused by vitamin B deficiency, for the food was still very bad. Some prisoners tried to escape by digging through the walls of the barns, but none got away.

One was shot as he emerged from the hole in the wall. All these fellows who were caught were confined in the pigsties in the farmyard in complete darkness and under lock and key. One or two of them died in these places. After a few days here another kommando of prisoners arrived and were put into one of the barns . . . our numbers having dwindled considerably. This new kommando stayed only a few days and we got a new line in refined cruelty. One of their German medical men used to take great delight in dosing fellows with belladonna which turned them blind for about twenty-four hours. He used to howl with laughter to see his victims groping their way about the yard.

Not only the men suffered. Conditions also deteriorated markedly in some of the *Offizierlager* in the early summer of 1918; it was as though, for the period in the wake of their successful offensives, the Germans felt that they no longer had to exercise restraint in the treatment of prisoners. Conditions in the officers' camp at Rastatt on the edge of the Black Forest, which had never been renowned for the standard of its accommodation or food, dropped even further into the depths in mid-1918. Typical German rations for the day comprised coffee and one-fifth of a loaf of brown German bread at 8 a.m., a bowl of soup at 12 noon, another bowl of soup at 6.30 p.m., and beetroot, or very rarely about four stewed figs, or sometimes three baked potatoes per man. The only hard thing on which to bite was the bread, so after a while the prisoners began to suffer from various tooth ailments, and the mostly liquid diet played havoc with their digestive systems. Captain McMurtrie of the Somerset Light Infantry found himself there in May 1918, and reported that:

> The sanitary conditions were awful. We barely had enough blankets on our beds to keep us warm during the colder days. There was one counterpane, two dirty blankets, a straw pillow and terribly hard straw mattresses. The Germans started a canteen charging outrageous prices, 1½d for one cigarette and the only food we could get were small biscuits about 2 inches in diameter and an eighth of an inch thick for which they charged 3d and there were very few to be obtained. . . . Very few people had any money and so most people could not buy anything. We were so starved that we ate raw turnips and carrots and some even ate the potato peelings. Hunger is a terrible thing and without books or any occupation it is Hell. Rastatt was the biggest Hell I have ever been in and to make matters worse every day we heard of huge German advances at Albert, Amiens and Kemmel . . . and then of Paris being threatened and then we began to see a far distant date – our return to England but not the England we knew, an England vanquished and crushed with Prussian Militarism ruling the world. It was not a nice position, for certainly, from the news we could get, the Allies seemed to be almost beaten.

Brigadier-General H. C. Rees also arrived at Rastatt on 2 June, and confirmed McMurtrie's impressions.

> At Rastatt, we continued to starve on the same rations, but were able to eke them out a little with a few biscuits, purchasable at the canteen. There was a good deal of sickness among the officers at Rastatt, owing to the food.

Despite the privations in the *Offizierlager*, it is doubtful whether McMurtrie or Rees or any of the others would willingly have changed places with the men in some of the crueller working camps or the mines, where raw turnips and carrots and potato peelings would have been welcome additives to the miserable starvation diet. Corporal C. E. Green of the Scots Guards, still labouring in the mines at Preussengrube in May 1918, reported that

> One of our sentries went mad. He was a young Polish fellow, and had been here over two years. . . . A Russian was killed down

below by an Oberhauer striking him on the head with a pick. The Pole stated that the dead man had on a suit of civilian clothes beneath his working clothes. But that was not the exact truth, I'll swear. . . . Still no parcels, and nearly everyone 'on the rocks'.

And, in July, Green reported the death of a young Englishman who was gassed in the mine, as well as the demise of

a lot of newly captured Englishmen dying in hospital. Too much German soup, followed by dropsy and death. One died today. Poor fellows, it is all they have to eat. . . . One young fellow here made four attempts to cut his throat. He said that he worked until he dropped and then the civilians started to thrash him.

One feature of the eastern mining camps in the summer of 1918 was the growing number of Russian escapes. The Armistice of November 1917, followed by the turmoil of the early months of the Bolshevik Revolution, convinced many Russian POWs that now was the time to make a bid for freedom. Fresh contingents of Russians were arriving all the time from the western front, where many had been employed in trench digging and other labouring activities for three years. Up to fifty Russians, Green records, were escaping every week.

In August 1918 the miseries of the POW and working camps were aggravated by a new horror: the first inroads of the great influenza pandemic which, by the spring of 1919, was to claim 27 million lives throughout the world. No one knows for certain where, or how, the pandemic started; according to some accounts it began in an overcrowded army barracks in Kansas, where 26,000 men were affected in March and April 1918. Those who recovered came to France with the American Expeditionary Force that summer, and acted as carriers of the virus. Another theory is that it originated in the rat-infested trenches of the French Army. Whatever the truth, it spread with appalling speed; in June 1918 it affected 160,000 people in Berlin alone. In the POW camps, it found easy prey among men in a terribly debilitated state. As Corporal Arthur Speight recalled:

You can imagine what a clean sweep it made amongst us in our miserable condition. There was no relief for sufferers, however, and many went out to work and never returned alive. One guard named Heinrich Klein was particularly horrible. He thrashed a lad called Saville so unmercifully that he died. Klein returned later and thrashed the body in an attempt to make it get up and do something. We reported this matter to the officer who said that it would be looked into. Klein was removed, but only to the quartermaster's store! I had an attack of influenza here and I am sure that I owe my life to Graefe [a German lance-corporal clerk] who used to save me part of his ration of stew, which though poor was infinitely better than ours. . . . Our physical condition and numbers had gone so far downhill now that we looked like disappearing altogether as a Kommando and my time was taken up with compiling lists of the men who had died.

No figures are available for the number of POWs who succumbed to the influenza virus. However, statistics are available for the British Expeditionary Force, and these give some idea of the pandemic's extent. Between 18 May and 10 August 1918, 226,615 soldiers were admitted to hospital suffering from the illness, and a further 87,323 were admitted during a second outbreak from October to December. Of these, 5,377 died.

Surprisingly, some of the worst-appointed POW camps escaped the influenza scourge. Captain McMurtrie reported that at Rastatt 'We were very lucky not to get any outbreaks of disease as I am sure half of us would have died owing to the very bad sanitary conditions and very weak state we were all in at that time.'

Early in June McMurtrie was transferred to Graudenz, which was different from the distribution camp at Rastatt in every sense. After parading on arrival,

We were put into a large mess room with trestle tables, all very nice and clean and all laid out with cups, saucers, plates and knives. Coffee and bread were given to us and we began to think that this was indeed the haven of rest we had dreamt and longed for at Rastatt. . . . We were taken to a room on the second floor of Block I. It was a good sized room with six beds, composed of an iron frame with four wooden boards stretched across and on top of these boards three funny looking 'spring mattresses', which were made of springs of a very sharp type with a thin covering of canvas around them. We were also given two good, clean white blankets, one much-worn sheet, a beautiful check counterpane and a very hard pillow also encased in a check covering. We had three separate cupboards, fitted with a long chest of drawers, meat safe and hanging compartment. . . . There were six hard wooden stools, one good table about one yard by three yards, one small table, about ten coat pegs and two good double windows. The outlook from the windows was quite pretty, across the valley some low-lying country with some heavily-wooded hills in the distance.

Graudenz, however, was virtually escape-proof, with plenty of barbed wire and double rows of sentries on either side, and the food did not match the scenery or the accommodation.

The food conditions immediately got very much worse, the bread ration was cut down to one-seventh and later one-eighth of a loaf a day and the soup got steadily thinner; as was bound to happen, we all got very weak. The worst time we had was the second week we were at Graudenz. We were so weak that we lay on our beds most of the day; it was only with a great effort that we could get up the three flights of stairs and when we did we were out of breath. Officers were often carried off from roll-call fainting and if we had got any epidemic at that time then certainly half of us would not have lived.

The canteen at first had very little in it, but later it produced some quite weird articles for the prisoners' consumption, including some 'obnoxious' jam, tinned mussels, 'most terrible stuff, but we ate it' and some fish salad, 'a green slimy mess of mussel fish and a weird sort of cabbage. The stuff appeared out of wooden barrels and smelt terrible.'

McMurtrie was critical of the messing arrangements; there appeared to be a flourishing racket in full swing here.

The messing from start to finish was very badly run by a messing committee of English officers. The messing committee and their friends got fat and the food, such as it was, was very unfairly distributed. Captain Moore and I saw the head of the messing committee and told him about the system, but things did not get any better and everyone was sick of it. Eventually Moore and I saw the Brigadier and told him about it. He gave the official 'I will look into it' and then did nothing. We had done our best to get the food fairly distributed and it was impossible to make any improvement and so all of us in Room 108 decided we would try to improve things on our own. We knew the officer who looked after the cookhouse and every day that we had a fairly good soup we took our kettle down and filled it with soup and then we brought it back to the room pretending it was full of hot water. . . . All the time office-holders used their appointments not for the good of the camp but their own benefit. As this was the case throughout the camp we felt justified in trying to help ourselves.

One *Offizierlager* in which food was abundant was Bad Colberg, about sixty miles from the Austrian border but some 300 from any neutral frontier. Practically all the 245 officers and 70 orderlies were receiving parcels from home, so there was plenty for everyone. Nevertheless, as reported by Brigadier-General Rees, who arrived there in July 1918, regulations were strict.

Before the war it had been a sanatorium, but as the company who owned it had gone bankrupt, the buildings were in bad repair. There were two buildings, the 'Main Building' and the 'Villa Peters', the two being connected by an alley of barbed wire. No-one was allowed to stand still in this alleyway; if one did, the sentries had orders to fire on one. Trivial offences against the camp regulations were punished with, usually, six days' cells, which meant confinement in the cellars under Villa Peters. As an illustration, to be met with at the hands of the commandant, one officer, who had converted a blanket of his own into a dressing gown, in which for months he had gone in to his bath in the morning, was given six days for 'being in possession of a civilian overcoat' and given no opportunity to state his case. Another officer, who tried to escape through the commandant's office was tried for 'house breaking' and given eighteen months' imprisonment for it as a civil offence.

After the disasters of the spring and early summer, the heartening news began to filter through to the camps that the German offensive had collapsed and that the initiative had passed to the Allies. Later came more heartening news that American forces in large numbers were now committed to the fighting, and from September there were persistent rumours that the Americans had succeeded in breaking through. One fact that gave credibility to these rumours was the absence of American prisoners of war; in fact, between the end of August and the beginning of November 1918 only 2,163 Americans were taken prisoner, a very low figure considering the number of US troops (600,000) in action against the enemy.

113

As the Allies once again took the offensive, many of the POWs who had been employed on working parties behind the German lines were suddenly moved to permanent camps in Germany. One of them was Corporal Arthur Speight, who was sent to Friedrichsfeld in October. Of the 2,000 men who had assembled as prisoners with him at Ramecourt in May, only 292 were still alive.

We were put into huts where we found lots of other British prisoners. They were astounded at our condition, and of all the parties coming in at that time, they said that ours was the worst they had seen. These fellows had a whip round as soon as we showed up in the morning and gave us food from parcels which had been sent to them from home. This was the first good food we had eaten since May 26 or 27th and it had very dire effects in several cases. I remember that I was fearfully sick that day. The huts at this camp were fairly good; they were about 100 feet long by say 30 feet wide. . . .

The camp was surrounded by a barbed wire fence about fifteen feet high. About ten feet outside this was an electrified wire netting about six feet high. Then came another barbed wire fence like the first and a deep moat, filled with water, round the outer edge of which the sentries patrolled. The sentries' beat was illuminated by means of powerful arc lamps and at each corner of the camp was a high platform surmounted by a machine gun which was manned all day and all night. . . .

No smoking was allowed in the huts. . . . It was an unwritten law that anyone noticing the approach of any German stepped into the hut and shouted 'Eyes down!' in a loud clear voice. All cigarettes were out before the German sergeant happened to get inside. One old German sergeant found this out and always used to shout 'Eyes down!' before he came in, which was very sporting of him. Our hut was in charge of a German corporal who had been wounded on the Somme and was the proud possessor of the Iron Cross. He also was a decent fellow and often came in for a smoke on the quiet.

Another prisoner who was moved into Germany in October 1918 was the anonymous diarist of Le Cornet Malo. He saw at first hand, *en route* to prison camp, the miserable deterioration of conditions among the German civilian population.

114

October 18. Still don't know where we are going. At one station where we stopped, a German girl about eight or nine years old came to the window and said 'Brot'. She was apparently asking us for bread and it struck me as being as good a mixture of humour and tragedy as one could get. Humorous, because we would have given anything for a piece of bread, and tragic, because the youngster, who was quite respectably dressed, should be reduced to asking prisoners of war for bread. Unfortunately, one of the guards heard her and he gave her a smack on the side of the face which sent her tumbling into some Germans who were standing near. I couldn't help wondering whether that youngster's father was fighting or whether he had gone the way of thousands more and been disposed of like those in the hole at Neuve Chappelle.

October 19. Arrived at Worms at 8.0 p.m. today and taken to prison camp. Haven't lain down since we left the fort and feel as though I should break in two pieces.

October 20. What a night! When we arrived last night we were given some soup and then went to sleep. About 10.30 p.m. there was a devil of a noise and about eight Jerries came and fetched everyone out of their bunk. We were counted, the room was inspected and then we were allowed to go back to sleep again. About 12.30 a.m. the same thing happened again and at 2.30 a.m. and 4.30 a.m. it was repeated. At 7.0 a.m. we were fetched out for breakfast. I found out afterwards that some Froggies had previously occupied this room and during the night they tunnelled under the yard and so on until they were out of the prison. About 40 of them escaped in this way and so the nightly visits were made to prevent a repetition. There are only English and French here, but there are hundreds of Ruskies in the compound adjoining. Today we had a haircut, bath and fumigation. This camp seems to be much cleaner, so perhaps we shall have some peace from the everlasting lice. The food is awful. Two water soups and twelve to a loaf a day. The only consolation is that we have no work to do.

As early as July 1918, there were rumours in the camps that, according to the word spread by troops returning from the front, the **German Army would rise in revolt if the war did not end by**

115

September. September came and the war did not end, but the signs of German collapse were everywhere, not least emblazoned across the pages of the German newspapers. The Allies were hammering through the supposedly impregnable defences of the Hindenburg Line, Bulgaria surrendered on the last day of September, and in the east Turkey was crumbling in disorder. In Germany and Austria, revolution was about to explode. The power keg was lit in Kiel on 4 November, when substantial elements of the German High Seas Fleet mutinied and declared a Sailors' Soviet. In the days that followed, revolutionary emissaries were despatched throughout Germany, proclaiming the death of the old Reich and the birth of a new socialist republic. Only then did the thousands of men in the POW camps fully realize that the defeat of Germany, of which they had dreamed for so long, was a reality; and they were faced with an uncertain and possibly dangerous immediate future.

Chapter 9

ARMISTICE

The uncertainty that came with the news of Germany's rapid collapse touched every man in prison camp. One of the best descriptions of it is given by Captain J. B. Sterndale Bennett, MC, of the 2nd (24th) South Wales Borderers, who had been captured on the Lys in April 1918 and who was imprisoned at Schweidnitz in Silesia.

On November 10 1918 I found myself looking again, for the first time for a year, down the unpleasant end of a machine-gun. The display of force was a little puzzling to the three hundred hopelessly non-combatant British officers still incarcerated in that disused Reformatory politely called a Lager. Only the vaguest rumours had reached us of the declaration of a Republic; but these were confirmed that Sunday afternoon by the half comic, half pathetic spectacle of our German guard ripping the Imperial eagles from their helmets and helping each other to cut off the epaulettes from their tunics. I am afraid that we stood and laughed at them, which made them furious.

Automatically they kept to their sentry posts, and we turned our inquiries to the custodian of the gate. He knew nothing, only that Wilhelm II had fled and, so far as he was concerned, no one had arisen to take his place. We could walk out of prison that moment for all he knew, but he advised patience, hinted darkly at an infuriated populace, and told us of the rumours (which lasted for some days) that bands of bloodthirsty sailors were expected hourly from Kiel. As we were many hundreds of miles from the Dutch frontier we accepted his advice to stay where we were and await results.

They came in the evening in the shape of a deputation from the Soldiers' and Workers' Council, headed by an unshaven, rat-like little man wearing a red armlet, who demanded to see our representatives. He issued his orders in a businesslike way, said that the life of the camp would proceed along the usual lines, except that he was, for our protection, installing a few machine-guns. There was no telling what the exasperated townspeople might do to us if they stormed the camp. Furthermore, we had better not show a head at any window after sunset. . . . But when the machine-guns arrived, they were pointed at us instead of at the expected desperadoes. One was at the bottom of the stairs trained on the only exit from our dormitories; one was on a raised slope levelled at the only exit to the courtyard.

It dawned on us gradually that the President of the Soldaten und Arbeiter Rat for some reason or other was frightened of us. But why? We had no special quarrel with him. We knew that the Armistice was virtually signed. We thoroughly welcomed his revolution, if only as light relief to a monotony which had paralysed us, in some case, for years. Besides, we had nothing to fight him with except chair legs and a few kitchen utensils.

We discovered later that it was well known that during the earlier Russian revolution German officer-prisoners had sided with Russian officers and shown some resistance to the revolutionary forces. It took us nearly a week, if I remember, to persuade the new authority that we did not care two straws what happened to their officers, for whom we had no great love. . . .

Our freedom was gradually extended. We were allowed to roam the town, cash our Cox's cheques at a ruinous rate of exchange and spend our money in the hotels and weinstuben. The repercussions of the Revolution, at this time, were extraordinarily interesting to watch. The terms of the Armistice were still regarded as some fantastic nightmare. Even in these early days there was intense disappointment that the end of the war had not been immediately followed by an amelioration of daily hardships.

Without the smallest sense of 'war guilt', the common German had persistent faith that the dismissal of the Kaiser would satisfy all the fiercest demands of his enemies. They were and had been for some years hungry and ill-clothed. They expected that the blockade would be immediately raised, that food would become readily available. I listened more than once to the bitter complaints of civilians that this had not been done. I could think of no other way of countering them than to point out that their censorship had never allowed their enemies to know of their pitiful plight. Pitiful enough it was, as anyone who was in that remote town in 1918 must have seen.

As our Red Cross supplies increased, we used to stuff our pockets with biscuits and chocolates and give them to the children, whose little cheekbones were prominent in their gaunt faces and who would follow us on our walks for miles, as though we were so many Pied Pipers.

In some camps, news of the revolution came as a surprise. One of them was Graudenz, as Captain McMurtrie recalls:

On Sunday November 10th, about 12 a.m., a German photographer came into the camp. . . . He told some people that a revolution was going to take place that day in Graudenz. We of course didn't believe him, but about 1 p.m. that day, we saw all the Boche officers and soldiers straggle on to the parade ground opposite. Some were seen to talk to the crowd and then the men got into three bunches and the officers remained alone. There were several shows of hands and then they all went away. Afterwards, we learnt that they had told the officers that their powers were suspended and then each company elected a representative. That night the officers came in to take roll-call in caps without the usual two cockades and without shoulder badges.

The next day . . . orders were issued by the Brigadier asking us not to make a row etc. and a wire was received from the English War Office advising us not to try to go home until the Boche made transport arrangements. On the Monday morning the Commandant appeared in 'mufti' and handed over the tin room almost crying. How are the mighty fallen. From then on we were given our parcels as soon as they came in, letters were not censored and a great many of the annoyances came to an end.

Revolutionary representatives visited Bad Colberg too, and as Brigadier-General Rees tells, caused some unintentional humour.

'As an outward and visible sign of revolution, a red flag was hoisted on the flag staff, the flag being made of two red pocket handkerchiefs borrowed from one of our orderlies. The interpreter,

supported by some curious looking citizens wearing armlets with
the words *Arbeiter-Soldaten Rat*, ended his harangue by saying,
'and we hope soon that we can you to Blighty send'. The speech
had been listened to with breathless interest, and his final
sentence was greeted with shouts of laughter and ironical cheers.

In the other ranks' POW camps the mood of jubilation following
the announcement of the Armistice generally overcame any hard
feelings that might have been harboured towards the guards. At
Friedrichsfeld, Corporal Arthur Speight and the other prisoners
were assembled for the evening roll-call on 10 November, where the
news was broken in simple terms by the German interpreter. 'I don't
want you to make much noise,' he said, 'but Germany has lost the
war and it is finished.'

Speight describes the following days:

The next morning, we found that some bold spirit had nailed a
Union Jack and a French flag to the tops of two arclight poles.
The Jerries were furious at this but I don't think they ever found
out who did it. There was a distinct change of atmosphere now.
Nobody would take any orders from the guards and some of the
guards themselves, especially those with the machine-guns,
packed up and went home. The German officers did not have
much hold on them now and this led to a visit by the officer
commanding the lager who was an old dug-up General or
something. He was furious at the slipshod way everything was
being done and when he was standing near our hut he was about
purple with indignation. He drew his sword, waved it round his
head, slammed it back in its scabbard and began to spit at
anyone who was near. . . .

The Germans now dropped us altogether as regards rations
and we had to live on the parcels which had been stored in a large
building in the lager. There was a small riot when some French
and Russians tried to raid this store but nothing very serious
happened. Our German corporal was also badly off for food so we
used to stand him his grub too. In return, he used to take us down
to the town of Wesel nearby, and armed with a tin of cocoa or a
couple of bars of Sunlight soap we used to descend on the pubs
which, for this price, would supply six men with beer for as long
as they cared to stay. The lager was visited every day by German
civilians begging for bully beef and biscuits.

One evening while we were sitting round our stove, a German soldier popped his head into our room and said: 'Hey! Is any o' ye b—s from Newcassel? We just said, 'Why howay in man,' and in he came. His name was Nägler, I think, and he said he had been a waiter at the County Hotel for several years. His wife belonged to Jesmond (a suburb of Newcastle-on-Tyne) and as he was going home we loaded him with tins of bully, jam, and as many biscuits as he could manage, whereupon the poor fellow cried like a child.

The sudden and complete change of attitude between the German officers and men was noticeable everywhere. On 10 November, the diary of the anonymous prisoner of Le Cornet Malo, now at Worms, records

Glorious news today. Armistice signed and we expect to leave shortly. What a difference in the attitude of the guards towards the officers. Yesterday they would spring to attention when the officer was a mile off, but today they treat him as though he wasn't there. Their attitude towards us is different too. They don't seem to mind what we do. For example, we broke down the 10 ft partition dividing us from the next camp and Jerry walked to the other end of the camp so that he should not see. When we got in the other camp I saw two men, or rather skeletons, because they were nothing more. They wore khaki clothes and looked ghastly. I asked them who they were and what regiment they belonged to, but they had lost all power of speech. I don't know whether they were British or not, but they must have been treated hellishly to be in that condition.

The Jerry NCO, who delighted in making us stand with our faces to the wall while he flourished his revolver and held forth about swiner Englanders and spat on the ground to show his hatred of us, has disappeared. Perhaps it's as well, because I feel sure some of the men now would give him a rough time.

The revolutionary Workers' and Soldiers' Council representatives apparently deemed it unnecessary to venture as far afield as the eastern mining camps to spread their gospel. At Preussengrube, Corporal Green reports, it was work as usual despite the news of the Armistice, although riots in Russian Poland caused some excitement, the rioters 'finding out all the rich Jews who have been hoarding up food. One house was raided, and in it was found 100 tons of meal, also bacon and other foodstuffs'.

Able Seaman Byrne and his colleagues did not learn of the Armistice until 22 November, when:

> As we were settling down for the night a messenger came to our barbed wire fence and pushed a note through it, which read as follows: 'Armistice signed November 11, if you are still being forced to work act accordingly, it is up to you to take action.'
>
> We knew what to do all right. We pushed everything we had behind the door inside the room and fastened the windows, and when the sentry came to fall us in for work he was surprised: even he didn't know that the Armistice was signed, so off he went into town and brought an Army sergeant to speak English to us. He said: 'If you will not work then you will not eat.' We said 'All right' but we did not take our barrage down, and the German knew that he couldn't force us to work now.
>
> The officer in charge of the local prison camp came to see us; he was very kind, although very stern. He tried to get us to work but we wouldn't give in, in spite of their threat to starve us. We managed to get food from some civilians – black bread, coffee and potatoes. We were kept locked in that room for three days, but used the windows to get out into the barbed wire enclosure at night. . . . After they let us loose in the enclosure things were cheerful, and they gave us some parcels that had come from England. They had been severely dealt with; nevertheless we were pleased to have them.
>
> After keeping us there for a week they took us back to HQ at Brandenburg. There we met almost all our pals and we had a merry do. The civilians in the city invited us to go down and make whoopee, but only a few went. Another man challenged any Englishman to a boxing match; one of our Naval boxers went down with three supporters. Our men were pretty fit so we expected a good fight. In came the German gang, strong-looking and smiling. Our man looked [the German boxer] up and down as he was putting on his gloves, and took no heed of anyone. The time was about 7 o'clock when the fight began. After it had been in progress for a few minutes the German was unrecognisable, while the Englishman was untouched. Of course this was not very pleasing to the Jerries; someone switched out the lights and there was a scatter. . . . Our men just managed to get away without being mauled.

The order to keep on working – sometimes with an offer of increased pay – was obeyed in a few places, but not in most. At Preussengrube, the Russian Poles were released on 15 November; they were simply marched over the frontier and then turned loose. Two days later, as Corporal Green records,

> Sunday once again, and the last one, I firmly believe, we shall spend under the present circumstances. From our windows we can see the German sentries patrolling the higher ground just outside our official residence. The Bolschewski Party of Polish fighters are making their advance towards Beuthen, and I think they will not be long in coming on to this place. . . . It is said that 120,000 Russians left Germany for their homes today. But there is no news about when *we* go.

> 18.11.18. The time of work was slightly altered, with I might say a great deal of satisfaction to all. The day shift is now from 6–2 p.m., and the late shift is 3–11 p.m. I am, however, still off work, and my present main object is to have the skies for a roof, not stone or coal. The Emergency Parcels were better than the former ones, except there was not enough to go round. One parcel to each man. But there were ten packets of Woodbines in each Regimental box.

At Friedrichsfeld, where the prisoners had been subjected to brutal treatment in the nearby mines, they were not in any mood to continue working for their erstwhile masters. Trooper Walter Jowsey of the Royal Horse Artillery tells how the mood of defeat was clearly apparent among the Germans in late October:

> They used to shout that they were beaten and there was a lot of talk of revolution, and that the Kaiser would have to go. They were in an awful state for food by now, and would offer us anything for bully beef or anything like that. You could get ten marks (about eight shillings) for a tin of bully beef, but we would never sell them it. They would see us starve, so we got a bit of our own back. Boots they had none; they would offer you thirty marks for a pair of old uppers, and they got wooden soles nailed on to these.
> On 9 November we went to work in the mine as usual. It was our double shift. When we got there they wouldn't let us go in, as they were on strike. The Revolution was on in Germany. They

said they wouldn't work until the Kaiser had cleared out and peace was declared. They broke into the place where the food was stored and looted our parcels from the truck that had just brought them up. . . .

On the tenth about 5,000 of them, including wives and families, marched with red flags flying to see the mayor of the next village about more food. The sentries at the camp then cleared off to join the revolutionaries. . . . We got dressed up and went for a walk in the town. We couldn't do anything wrong for the Germans, now that the English were good etc. and would send them plenty of food. We thought 'I don't think!' but we didn't tell them that. On Monday the 11th we got to know of the Armistice and went to work until Thursday, when we went on strike. The civilians backed us up; they would do anything for us now. Nobody but the prisoners will know how the Germans were starving. Dozens died every week in our village alone from hunger.

In Belgium, where considerable numbers of British prisoners were still employed on working parties, the news of the Armistice was accompanied by a degree of confusion. Belgian flags appeared everywhere; the Germans hoisted red flags and their troops were bedecked with red ribbons. Initially the Germans tried to exercise a measure of control over the POWs, but this was soon abandoned. As Private Reginald Bellamy recalls, everyone, British and German alike, was now in the same big melting-pot; they shared billets in Belgian houses and generally got on reasonably well together. Time and again, the British were astonished by the sudden and complete transformation in the Germans' attitude and temperament now that the shooting was over; it was almost as if four years of war had never been.

The POWs got no further rations from the Germans but were well supplied by the principal Belgian relief organization, the Comité Nationale; the Belgian civilians, too, were free in their gifts of food, and in the use of their homes. Bellamy's diary for 15 November reads:

Went out this morning and met a boy who was looking for someone who wanted a billet. He took us home with him to No. 86 Rue de la Station [in Waremme] and we are in a little palace. A room to ourselves – and beds! A good dinner! Clean shirts and trousers!

The young lady looks after us very well. Had a good wash. . . .
Seems all impossible.

The prisoners at first had thought of making for Holland, but with
the treatment they were receiving decided it was better to stay where
they were and wait until Allied troops arrived. In the mean time, the
former prisoners relaxed, went for walks, and played football with
the locals. On 25 November:

The first body of Allied troops in the shape of French cavalry
arrived about noon. They received a great welcome. . . . They
looked very smart in their blue uniforms and steel helmets, but
their horses, many of whose harnesses were decorated with
flowers, looked none too well. One old woman of 60 or so had
hold of a Frenchman's hand and was dancing along mad with
joy.

At Schweidnitz in Silesia, as Captain Sterndale Bennett reports,
the revolution came and went without undue commotion.

The townspeople, being some considerable distance from Berlin,
were by no means certain at that time which way the cat would
jump. . . . Every German gasthof or hotel of importance in those
days gave a place of honour to two framed portraits, one of 'Old
Fritz' (Frederick the Great) and one of Wilhelm II. The careful
proprietors, at the Revolution, did not remove them; they covered
them with brown paper to be ripped off at the first sign
of a Royalist reaction. The licentious sailors never came to
Schweidnitz.

The little town weathered its revolution without a shot fired.
. . . If one accepts it that bloody revolutions are nurtured in
hunger, they had every excuse for violence, but the sound
common sense of the middle class prevailed. . . . Another feature
of the German psychology which must have helped them was
their abhorrence of the crime of theft – and more particularly at
this time of the theft of food. . . . There was attached to the camp
an elderly German doctor, in uniform, but still in practice in the
town. We also had, as a fellow prisoner, a doctor in our own
RAMC. The two worked together, and when the case [of medical
stores] was opened the jealous eye of the old German fell on two
luxuries which he had not seen for many months – a tin of boracic
powder and a tin of cocoa. He later stole them, was detected by

his own orderly, who bore him some grudge, and reported via the English doctor to the German Commandant. He was court-martialled and dismissed his post.

We received, I suppose, roughly 75 per cent of the parcels sent to us. Of the missing 25 few were stolen in Germany. There was a leakage, I have been told, before they ever left this country [England]. Mostly they disappeared in Holland. Certainly, once they had been handed over, no German touched them. [This might have been true in Schweidnitz: it was certainly not the case elsewhere.]

The four weeks after the Armistice were not the unhappiest in our lives. They were a prelude to a larger liberty – and our first opportunity of seeing anything of the life of the country at that time. A certain fraternization was inevitable. Most of us had scraps of the language, some were fluent. One of my fellow prisoners became persona grata in a German family. Others must have done the same if our send-off was any criterion. As we assembled at the station to entrain for Danzig the station yard was full of smiling inhabitants, many of whom had brought flowers, and they gave us a rousing cheer as we started on our long journey.

Inevitably, there was a small minority who viewed the prospect of going home with misgiving. There were those who had collaborated with the Germans to an excessive degree, and others who had resorted to habitual petty crime in the confines of prison camp. Still others had different reasons, as Private Preston of the KRRC recounts. At Langensalza:

We received army instructions to stay put at the mine until further notice. We were told to report for work as usual and if we refused the Germans had to deny us food until we succumbed. One concession we got was complete liberty to walk about anywhere. We all had a conference in the largest room in the barracks and decided to obey the orders in the hope that they made haste to return us to England.

There was one objector about going home. He was one of three men who used to come to us on Sunday afternoons to talk and play cards. These three men came from separate farms where they worked and they had freedom to walk about wherever they liked. This chap said he didn't want to go home because, living in

Manchester before the war, he had been a drop-out, very idle and of no use to his family or society. But since he had been on the farm he had learnt all about sugar beet growing and general farming and now had the basis of a useful career. He had never been as happy in his life. He spoke quite openly of the fact that the farmer had to serve at the front and eventually he started sharing the farmer's bed with the farmer's wife. We understood his meaning and told him he could please himself, realizing that we would have our own problems to sort out after being away from home for five years.

In general, the great homeward movement from the camps got under way during the third week of November, the German authorities having been made responsible for the provision and assembly of transport. The anonymous prisoner of Le Cornet Malo left Worms in some style on a river boat on 20 November, as his diary records:

At last we are away. The barrack rooms were being gradually burnt and the Froggies were getting more impatient than we were. The boat left about 1.0 p.m. and we stayed at Engelheim for the night. . . . 21 November. Left Engelheim at 8 o'clock this morning and enjoyed the trip. Came down the noted Rhine valley and could have appreciated it better in different circumstances. Passed Coblenz and arrived at Cologne about 6.0 p.m., staying here the night. . . . 23 November. Left Cologne at 7.30 this morning. Saw the Cathedral and many other fine buildings as we passed. Reached Düsseldorf about 1.0 p.m. There seemed to be an unending stream of German transport passing over the bridge. . . . 24 November. We didn't travel far yesterday, but that was probably due to the fact that we are in Holland.

At Friedrichsfeld, the first hint that the move was about to start came when representatives of the Dutch authorities visited the camp to make the travelling arrangements. The prisoners were split up into manageable parties and the first of these left almost immediately. Arthur Speight, because of his ability as an interpreter, stayed on for another fortnight until all the prisoners who were too sick to make the homeward journey were sent to a proper hospital. Then he too departed, with the last batch of fifty men, marching through the camp gates and down to Wesel where they boarded a train that took them to Zevenaar, just over the Dutch border. Here they left the train and were given a good meal, after which they boarded another train bound for Rotterdam, arriving at the Waterside Station after dark. They marched through the city and spent the next two days in a large warehouse on the dockside until at last a ship – the LMS ferry *Londonderry* – arrived to take them home. As Speight recalls:

We were all given a small flag and a bar of chocolate when we went aboard. We lay off the Hook of Holland all night. The next day was very foggy so we were unable to proceed, but on the next we crossed over to Cromer where we lay all night. Early next morning we entered the Humber, passing through lines of torpedo boats and drifters, all of which gave us a grand howl on their whistles. It made one's back hair curl to hear this rousing welcome. The food on the ship was a dream; bread and butter, tinned rabbit and bottles of stout at each meal. We landed at the Riverside Station at Hull and boarded a train for Ripon, from whence I was demobbed. I arrived in Sunderland on 10 December, looking quite plump and absolutely giving the lie to all my tales of misery.

Brigadier-General Rees also arrived at Hull, but only after a great deal of frustration and delay. After the announcement at Bad Colberg that the Armistice had been signed, nothing happened for five weeks. The prisoners lived on rumours; telegrams sent by the senior British officers to various authorities went unanswered, and to make matters worse the weekly food parcels ceased to arrive. In the end Rees was asked by the SBO at Bad Colberg, General Dawson, to go to Berlin in person to find out what was causing the hold-up. The German camp commandant was reluctant to agree to this, but changed his mind when the British officers threatened him with reprisals.

Rees and another officer named Campbell – a first-rate linguist who spoke German, French, and Russian fluently – set off for Berlin accompanied by a German *Feldwebel*. They travelled via Coburg and Lichtenfels, where they were lucky enough to catch the first train from Munich to Berlin since the Armistice. (It was now 12 December.) Rees admitted that he was by no means anxious to go to Berlin as it was generally reported to be the scene of constant street fighting and he had no wish to be shot in a street brawl after surviving the war.

However, the trouble in Berlin was grossly exaggerated and I saw no rioting whilst we were there. We arrived about 10 p.m. The station was crammed with soldiers and beyond the fact that our Feldwebel was ordered by a representative of the Soldiers' Council to take off his sword, we were not interfered with at all.

We drove in a Landau to the Adlon Hotel and there met a Mr Enderis, an American on the Associated Press. He told us that the British Red Cross delegates lived at the Esplanade Hotel so we went there, rather over-fortified by some Scotch whiskey which he produced in our honour. At the Esplanade we met a Mr Mayne, who was acting head of the Red Cross in Berlin. . . . The 13th December I spent interviewing Mayne and Sir Edward Ewart, who had just arrived from Basle, with a view to getting our camp moved. I couldn't get anything definite. Mayne was moving camps east of the Elbe and wouldn't make any definite offer. Eventually, I saw the Netherlands Minister, Van Rapart, who I found had the matter in hand and who arranged with the Council of Six for the camp to leave on the 24th. I fixed up with the officer in charge of supplies to send the camp some food, so the object of my visit to Berlin was accomplished.

During the day, Campbell and I saw the [German] Guards march into Berlin. It was a pitiful display from the military point of view. The companies were only some 90 to 100 strong, mostly composed of very young boys and men. The machine gun limbers behind each company were drawn by the most sorry-looking nags I've ever seen and the guns were often rusty. All the men, horses and guns were bedecked with flowers, but there was no cheering.

Rees and Campbell spent a couple of days sightseeing in Berlin, and then departed by train for The Hague. On 18 December they arrived at Hull, having sailed from Rotterdam, paid a short visit to the dispersal centre at Ripon, and then travelled overnight to the War Office in London, where they spent the whole of the next day compiling a report on the state of affairs in Berlin.

Prisoners from the camps in the east were generally repatriated by way of Danzig, their ships crossing the North Sea to dock at Leith, the port of Edinburgh. Captain Sterndale Bennett described his own home-coming:

We landed at Leith on Christmas morning. Nothing could have exceeded the warmth of our welcome home. Our dear Edinburgh hostesses must have risen at the screech of dawn to have prepared the sumptuous breakfast which was laid out in the quayside sheds. The band of the Gordon Highlanders had turned out to play us ashore.

The first of our comapny to land that morning, I think by a universal wish of all aboard, was that very gallant sailor Captain Blaikie. [While in command of the SS *Caledonia* on 4 December 1916, Captain Blaikie had fired on a U-boat which attacked his ship. The *Caledonia* was sunk and her captain taken prisoner. It was announced in Germany that he would be shot, but eventually the German government, fearing reprisals, altered their decision.] We were moved that day to Scarborough, where in one of the fine hotels we were entertained to a magnificent Christmas dinner. In the morning we were medically inspected and given three documents, and open cheque for £2, a chit for two months' leave, and facsimile letter from the King.

Corporal Green, Private Preston, and Able Seaman Byrne came home via Danzig and Leith, as did Captain McMurtrie. At Graudenz, 200 officers were warned to be ready to leave on Saturday 23 November, but the departure date was put back at the last minute until the following Tuesday, much to everyone's annoyance. There was some consolation in the fact that everyone was now allowed into town without a guard. As McMurtrie recalled:

> We all went. Going into hotels and restaurants, Boche waiters would rush up and take your gloves, cap and coat. The hotel we went to was full of English officers and not a Boche in sight. I almost thought I was back in an officers' club in France. It was priceless being able to walk where we liked without a guard and it was very hard to get used to it.

On Tuesday afternoon, the camp was ordered to parade at 8.15 p.m. The officers sold all their remaining food to the Germans, packed their belongings in suit-cases made from the cardboard of Red Cross parcels and marched down to Graudenz station, which

> We left very, very happy about 10.30 p.m. that night in 2nd and 3rd class carriages. We had a slow, uncomfortable journey and arrived outside Danzig about 9 a.m. We then shunted around for

about three hours and at last got to the quay and detrained. A large liner was ready and when the Privates had got on board the officers went on with the ship's band playing 'Let's all go down the Strand.'

Foley, Ashby and I shared a 'top-hole' little cabin and we entered civilization once more. There were several Danish Red Cross nurses on board and one Scottish nurse. The liner was the SS *Russ* of the Danish Line, which before the war took emigrants to Canada. It was a boat of 8,500 tons and was very steady. It had been lent to the Russian Navy as an auxiliary cruiser at the outbreak of war, and had been in the hands of the Bolsheviks up to a week before. It had then been handed over in a filthy state. Within six days it had been painted throughout, newly furnished and overhauled. Here then we first had fresh food, served very well, with table cloths, as many spoons, knives and forks as you wanted, comfortable chairs, good beer; no wonder some people were ill.

Most of the men, such as Reginald Bellamy, who had been employed on work details in Belgium, were on their way home by the end of November, usually travelling via Calais. Bellamy, who reached the port after a tiresome rail journey through Tirlemont, Louvain, and Brussels, came through the Flanders front, which was awful. Mud and desolation! After getting on to French ground soon rattled along and on arrival at Calais were taken to No 6 Rest Camp, had tea and were put in tents.' On 2 December, after a rough Channel crossing, Bellamy reached Dover to a tremendous reception from the vessels in the harbour, then entrained for a dispersal camp at Canterbury. The last entry in his diary – 5 December – aptly sums up his feelings, and those of thousands of fellow ex-prisoners: 'Arrived home tonight. Simply lovely.'

The repatriation of French, Belgian, Italian, and Portuguese POWs presented few logistical problems, once the necessary transport had been assembled. With the Russians, however, it was a different and far sadder story.

When the Treaty of Brest-Litovsk was finally signed between the Soviets and the Central Powers in March 1918, the Germans and Austro-Hungarians still held well over one million Russian prisoners, and their early repatriation was discussed at length during the prolonged negotiations. In the weeks that followed the repatriation process was started under the auspices of the German, Austro-Hungarian, and Russian Red Cross missions, and for some months there was a steady two-way traffic of home-coming POWs across the eastern frontiers. Immediately before the Armistice of November 1918, however, the rising tide of revolution in Germany, which brought an abrupt end to relations between Russia and the Central Powers, caused the repatriation process to break down completely.

The result was that hundreds of thousands of Russian POWs who were still in central Europe attempted to move eastwards unaided. Thousands died *en route* from starvation and disease; thousands more turned in their tracks and went back to the former prison camps, only to find that the barracks had been burned and that there was no food. Poland became a vast refugee camp for ragged, starving Russians with nowhere to go, and the problems were compounded by a westward flow of thousands of Austro-Hungarians who were straggling back from Russia.

The Red Cross missions did what they could. Their emissaries negotiated with the authorities in Poland, Lithuania, Czechoslovakia, Austria, Hungary, and Romania, through whose territories the masses of utterly destitute and hopeless men were wandering in both directions. The first priority was to feed them; the second, to organize their evacuation in manageable groups. The gigantic task went on through the spring of 1919, and involved the whole of the Red Cross structure in Europe, as well as other relief organizations. The British Red Cross and the Order of St John contributed foodstuffs to the value of £1,500,000, while British Red Cross missions – sometimes composed of former British officers who had themselves been prisoners of war – visited the camps in Germany where large numbers of Russians still existed in conditions of filth and misery. These Red Cross workers performed miracles in persuading the Russians to clean up the camps while awaiting repatriation.

Eventually, the camps in Germany were cleared. With the Russian Revolution in full swing, and an Allied Expeditionary Force now openly assisting the White Russians in fighting the Bolsheviks, the prospect of more organized repatriations of the Russians from the west had disappeared. The former POWs were therefore transferred to internment camps in the United Kingdom, France, and elsewhere and presented with the choice of making a new life outside their homeland. Many took advantage of the offer and travelled to the Far East, where they joined White Russian refugee colonies in Hong Kong and Shanghai; others settled in Western Europe and the Americas. But many more elected to return to Russia, and an uncertain future. To this day their fate remains unknown; and no one can say how many met their deaths before Bolshevik firing squads simply because, having fought in the Tsar's armies and then spent years in foreign camps, they were classed as politically unreliable.

Chapter 10

GERMAN PRISONERS
IN BRITAIN

In the early weeks of the First World War, the speed and success of the German advance on the Western Front meant that relatively few of their troops were captured by the Allies. Those who were taken were often uhlans or other mounted reconnaissance elements, surrounded during a foray into Allied territory. In fact, the first notable haul of German prisoners by the British occurred at sea, during the Battle of the Heligoland Bight on 28 August 1914, when 348 German survivors were taken aboard British warships. Of these, 224 – including the son of Admiral von Tirpitz, Chief of the German Imperial Naval Staff – were rescued from the light cruiser *HIMS Mainz*. Initially, therefore, it was civilian internees who comprised the main population of the British prisoner-of-war camps, although admittedly many of them were merchant seamen whose vessels had been taken as legitimate war prizes in various ports under British jurisdiction.

At the outbreak of war, Great Britain, in common with all the other belligerents, had no plan or machinery for dealing with large numbers of prisoners of war. The sole guide that existed for their reception and subsequent treatment was a Royal Warrant for the Maintenance of Discipline, dated 3 August 1914, which dealt in the main with the scale of punishments to be meted out to prisoners who did not conform to the rules. In fact, the document had its origin in a similar Royal Warrant that had been prepared during the Boer War, although the latest edition had a number of amendments incorporated in it.

Prisoners of war arriving in the United Kingdom were processed by a department of the Adjutant-General's Office, which was directly responsible to the War Office and became known simply as

AG 3. As there were no prison camps as such in the beginning, a great deal of improvisation was necessary; the first batches of prisoners were placed in existing army camps and barracks, modified for the purpose by the simple addition of barbed wire perimeters and machine-gun posts, and as a temporary measure some civilians were detained in prisons, although they were kept apart from the normal inmates. This was a Home Office, rather than a War Office, decision; although both were responsible for handling civilian internees, it was the Home Office which had the final say. One of the problems in creating adequate accommodation for POWs at this stage was that the British Army, in the autumn of 1914, suddenly found itself in the throes of a massive expansion programme, and as a consequence needed to extend its own military accommodation; the provision of prison camps as such was a secondary consideration.

The first prisoners to arrive in the United Kingdom in August 1914 were sent to a hastily converted army camp at Dorchester, and this was the first to be made into a permanent POW camp. Other permanent camps were also established in August at Queensferry (Flintshire) and Lancaster, while temporary camps were set up at Horsham, York Castle, Bradford Moor, Olympia (London), Edinburgh, and Fort George (on the Moray Firth). Some of these, however, were of a very temporary nature and were closed as soon as other permanent camps became available in September. One of these was at Frith Hill, Frimley; it was visited by a *Times* reporter, who described the inmates as

> Uhlans with riding breeches and spiked helmets, infantrymen in uniforms of blue-green, sailors in navy blue and civilians in the garb in which they had been arrested – one with a white waistcoat which he had been wearing at a wedding party when taken.

The prisoners amused themselves, he said, by playing games and listening to music.

For the civilian internees, a large camp was established at Knockaloe, on the Isle of Man; it was to remain the principal internment camp for the duration of the war. There was another POW camp on the Isle of Man, at Douglas. Other main military POW camps established during the closing months of 1914 were at Stobs in Argyll, where a major camp complex was set up;

Alexandra Palace in London; Handforth in Cheshire; Eastcote in Northamptonshire; Lofthouse near Wakefield; and Oldcastle in County Meath. As an additional measure, nine merchant vessels of the SS *Canada*, SS *Ascania*, and SS *Invernia* class – all of 4,000–5,000 tons – were requisitioned for use as prison-ships; when news of this reached Germany it caused a major outcry and led to allegations that German POWs were being subjected to harsh and brutal treatment. In fact the captives on board the ships were fairly comfortably housed, although they suffered from a lack of exercise and recreational facilities. Nevertheless, the use of the ships undoubtedly provided fuel for the German propaganda machine, and gave the Germans justification, from their outlook, for carrying out limited reprisals against British prisoners of war. The practice of confining POWs on the ships eventually ceased in June 1915.

The closing weeks of 1914 saw a welter of accusation and counter-accusation by both sides concerning the treatment of prisoners of war. As British and German interests in this respect were then being looked after by the United States, the US Ambassador in Berlin, J. W. Gerard – whose observers had already made a fact-finding tour of some of the POW camps in Germany – sought the approval of the British government to send his secretary, John B. Jackson, to the United Kingdom on a similar inspection tour. After some negotiation the necessary approval was forthcoming and, during the winter of 1914–15, Jackson was authorized to visit all the prison camps in Britain – there were then thirteen – as well as the nine prison-ships. By the time he completed his report in April 1915 the number of prisoners on British soil had risen to 26,000, of whom about 19,000 were civilians.

Jackson

Was given every opportunity of seeing everything, and of finding out anything if there were anything to find out. He conversed with the prisoners, and listened to all they had to tell him; there was no supervision, dictation, or interference of any sort by the British authorities during these talks; Mr Jackson and the prisoners were left absolutely to themselves, and he got at what was really in their minds. Twice he had luncheon with German officer prisoners, no British officer or soldier being present. Without exception the German officers assured him that they had always been treated as 'Officers and gentlemen' by the British.

He discovered that while in their camps these officers did practically what they pleased, and that there was no direct contact between them and the British officers and soldiers on guard, except when they were outside the wire enclosure.

Speaking of the camps generally, Mr Jackson noted that the German prisoners did their own police and fatigue work. He observed that the Frith Hill Camp, at Frimley near Aldershot, the prisoners ran their 'own little republic under their non-commissioned officers', who were responsible to the British military authorities, and that they had their own police, 'even their secret police'. At all camps opportunities were given for exercise, which, however, was not obligatory, although prisoners were expected to spend so many hours daily outside their sleeping quarters.

In these early days, no form of work or employment – except necessary tasks within the camps – was provided for the prisoners. Soldiers who had no uniforms were permitted to wear civilian clothes, and civilians who did not have the means to buy items such as clothing, shoes, and blankets received a government issue. Prisoners were also permitted books published in English and other languages before the war, and from January 1915 were also allowed British newspapers. Prisoners were allowed to send and receive two letters each week, a ruling that also applied – at least in theory – to British POWs in Germany. Their food, if not quite up to the standard of the basic British Army ration, was very nearly so; the daily POW ration comprised 1½ lb bread or 1 lb biscuit, 8 oz fresh or frozen meat or 4 oz pressed meat, ½ oz tea or 1 oz coffee, ½ oz salt, 2 oz sugar, $\frac{1}{36}$ oz pepper, $\frac{1}{20}$ lb condensed milk, 8 oz fresh vegetables, and 1 oz butter or margarine, with 2 oz cheese allowed as an alternative to the latter. This basic diet remained unchanged until January 1916, when food shortages made necessary a reduction in the bread ration.

The only complaints recorded by John Jackson during his inspection tour came from some civilians who had been taken from neutral ships or arrested in the colonies, although these were mainly concerned with the manner of their arrest and their treatment before being brought to the internment camps. Jackson's report concluded with the statement:

On the whole, the present treatment seems to be as good as could be expected under the circumstances. The new camps are all better than the old ones, and everywhere there seemed to be an intention to improve on existing conditions. Lack of organization and preparation would account for most of the hardships which prevailed at first. Absolutely nowhere did there seem to be any wish to make the conditions any harder or more disagreeable for the prisoners than was necessary, and I saw no instance, and heard of none, where any prisoners had been subjected to intentional personal annoyance or undeserved discipline.

Mr Jackson's findings tended to be corroborated by two representatives of the International Red Cross in Geneva, who toured the POW camps in Britain in February 1915 and reported no cases of dissatisfaction. These reports, however, were made before the notorious decision to segregate and imprison U-boat crews in April 1915 (see chapter 6), which caused a great deal of unrest not only in Berlin, but also among German POWs in the United Kingdom. Matters only improved when the submariners were released from prison in June 1915 and sent to normal POW camps, of which the principal one was Dyffryn Aled, near Denbigh in North Wales.

With experience, the organization for dealing with German prisoners of war gradually became more efficient in 1915. In February, the responsibility for processing them passed from AG 3 to a new department, the Directorate of Prisoners of War, under Lieutenant-General Sir Herbert Belfield, who had been in charge of AG 3. His deputy was Captain (Temporary Major) R. N. W. Larking.

These two officers and a small team worked tirelessly throughout 1915 to process and disperse the ever-growing numbers of POWs who were arriving in Britain. By the end of the year the number of established camps had increased to twenty-one in England, two on the Isle of Man, two in Scotland, one in Ireland, and one in the Channel Islands. There were also forty-two detention barracks, eight for military, six for naval, and twenty-eight for civilian prisoners; these were designed to house men who, for offences in prison camp or escape attempts, had been sentenced by due process of military or civil law to various terms of imprisonment. Civilian internees still formed the great majority of prisoners; in December 1915 there were 32,272 of them, compared with 12,349 military and 1,147 naval prisoners.

The Allied offensives of 1916 resulted in a vast increase in the number of German military prisoners, while repatriation lowered the number of civilian internees to around 31,000. The total of German Army prisoners of war on the last day of 1916 stood at 48,572, with a further 1,316 naval prisoners. The number of camps had also increased to thirty-eight in England, eight in Scotland, two in the Isle of Man, one in the Channel Islands, and one in Ireland; to take some of the pressure off the camps in the United Kingdom two large temporary POW camps were also established in France; although these were intended to be primarily collection and distribution camps, some German prisoners in fact spent a considerable time there until the camps were eliminated in the course of 1917. In the United Kingdom the number of detention centres also increased during 1916, with the swing now in favour of military offenders; there were twenty-four military detention barracks, twenty civilian, and fourteen naval.

Early in 1917 the Directorate of Prisoners of War was again expanded and its staff substantially increased. Colonel (Temporary Brigadier-General) T. E. O'Leary was appointed Deputy Director, while Brevet Major (Temporary Lieutenant-Colonel) Larking was appointed Assistant Adjutant-General. Until now the Directorate had, to some extent, assisted in handling the affairs of British prisoners of war, but this responsibility was now transferred entirely to the Red Cross.

By this time the German U-boat offensive against British merchant shipping was taking a heavy toll, with a resulting serious shortage of foodstuffs, and restrictions were placed on the rations available to POWs. From 19 February 1917, items containing sugar, jam, syrup, and flour, as well as meat, game, and poultry, were no longer permitted to be sold in canteens or otherwise made available for purchase by prisoners. The rule applied equally to military and civilian prisoners, except in the case of those who, for various reasons, drew no rations. These prisoners were allowed to purchase up to 2½ lb meat, ¾ lb sugar, and 4 lb bread a week, which was roughly equivalent to the ration allowed for British civilians under the regulations drawn up by the government food controller.

The number of German prisoners in the United Kingdom almost trebled during 1917 as a result of Allied successes, culminating in the British attack at Cambrai in November. At the end of the year there were 118,864 German and 9 Austrian military prisoners, 1,635

German and 1 Turkish naval prisoners, and civilian internees comprising 25,120 Germans, 4,065 Austrians, 108 Turks, and 223 others. There were now 142 prisoner-of-war camps in England, fourteen in Scotland, and one in Ireland. The number of military detention barracks had increased to thirty-three, but naval detention barracks had gone down to five, while those for civilian prisoners had also decreased to nine. In general, the number of offences in prison camp – both military and civilian – had declined during the year, possibly because widespread use was now being made of prisoners on labour duties outside the camps.

It was not until 1916 that German prisoners of war had been employed on external work in the United Kingdom. This was not because of any unduly lenient attitude in this respect by the British government – after all, it was known that British POWs had been employed in mines and other industrial concerns, as well as on the land, almost from the start of hostilities, and often under appalling conditions – but rather because civilian concerns in Britain showed a marked reluctance to use German prisoners. By 1917, however, attitudes changed; the manpower shortage in Britain was critical, and prejudices did not keep the wheels of industry turning.

The year 1917 therefore saw the first use of German POW labour on a very large scale nationwide, and by that autumn the POW labour force numbered some 70,000 men. This total included about 2,000 non-commissioned officers, who received a small pay increase for their efforts. Officers and senior NCOs were, of course, exempt from labour duties under the Hague Convention.

The tasks undertaken by the German labour force were many and varied. It is probably no exaggeration to say that the harvest of 1917 could not have been gathered in without the efforts of 30,000 German prisoners, distributed in labour gangs throughout the country under the supervision of 350 agricultural committees in a massive operation under the direction of the Ministry of National Service; after the corn was in they picked potatoes. Other POWs were employed in construction work, timber cutting, road building, and land reclamation; much of the agricultural land of East Anglia's fen country owes its existence to German labour.

The Directorate of Prisoners of War was hard put to cope with the massive influx of prisoners arriving in the United Kingdom after the collapse of the German 1918 spring offensives and the subsequent Allied counter-offensives. By October, the number was to exceed

250,000, and to accommodate them temporary camps mushroomed all over the country, so that in the autumn of 1918 there were no fewer than 492 in England, twenty-five in Scotland and one in the Channel Isles. The camp at Oldcastle in County Meath had been dismantled; with the Irish troubles on the increase, the presence of large numbers of German prisoners in Ireland had been viewed as a major security risk. In addition, thirty-five special hospitals – or sections of existing hospitals – were established for the treatment of enemy sick and wounded.

In June 1918 the POW ration scale was again reduced. The daily ration was now 9 oz bread and 4 oz broken biscuit, with meat (usually horse-flesh) on three days a week. There was also a twice-weekly issue of 1⅗ oz bacon, and 10 oz salt-cured, smoked, or pickled herrings. The remainder of the daily ration comprised tea (¼ oz) or coffee (½ oz), sugar (1 oz), salt (¾ oz), potatoes (20 oz), fresh vegetables (4 oz), split peas or beans or rice (1 oz), oatmeal (1 oz), jam (1 oz), cheese (1 oz), maize meal (1 oz), and pepper (¹⁄₁₀₀ oz). An additional weekly ration comprised either ½ lb salt-cured, smoked, or pickled herrings and 2 oz oatmeal, or 4 oz salt-cured, smoked, or pickled herrings, 2 oz broken biscuit, and 2 oz oatmeal. From March 1918 officers – who were not issued with rations, but received pay with which to buy them – were permitted to purchase 20 oz meat, 20 oz fish, and 56 lb bread a week.

The German rank and file were able to supplement their basic rations with Red Cross parcels from home, although as the food situation in Germany became desperate this source of supply became increasingly sporadic. They did, however, receive pay for the work they performed outside the camp, and with this they could buy extras such as fruit and tobacco at the camp canteens (where, doubtless, there were flourishing rackets, as in POW and internment camps in Germany). Under the Hague Convention wages earned by prisoners were to be used in the main to improve their position, and the balance paid over to the prisoner on release. In the United Kingdom, employers were charged for the services of prisoners at normal local hourly rates; they paid the full amount to the British authorities, who gave the prisoners an allowance under the terms set out in the Royal Warrant and credited the remainder against 'cost of maintenance'. In general, a POW's pay was between a halfpenny and twopence an hour, but those engaged in agricultural work could earn as much as a shilling an hour.

141

In many respects, German other ranks enjoyed a better and healthier life in British POW camps than did their officers. In the early days of the war the latter were given a free ration issue, but were later made to pay for it by having two shillings and twopence deducted daily from their pay, which was half that of a British infantry officer of corresponding rank and which consequently did not amount to a great deal, at least where junior officers were concerned. Officers were also expected to clothe themselves out of what was left, in addition to purchasing extras.

One of the most famous officer POW camps in England was Donington Hall, near Derby, once the ancestral home of the Hastings family. One German officer wrote that

> Donington Hall was supposed to be the model camp for the whole of England. According to the accounts we had been reading for weeks in the English papers it would seem to be a paradise on earth. Every day you might read columns on the subject, attacking the government for housing the prisoners too luxuriously. As usual, the women were the most violent, and had gone to the length of making the compulsory evacuation of Donington Hall a question for the women of England. Even in Parliament the subject was brought forward more than once.
>
> It was said that the place was furnished like a palace, with card-rooms and several billiard-rooms, that the game in the park was strictly reserved for the prisoners, and that even hunting was arranged for them. None of this was true. Donington Hall was a fine old seventeenth-century castle, certainly, and surrounded by a magnificent park; but the rooms were entirely bare of ornament, and the furnishing the scantiest and most primitive imaginable. Not a trace of billiards or card-room or hunting. But everything was spotlessly clean, and the commandant took admirable care that it should be. . . . Life at Donington Hall was almost the same as at Holyport, except that here we had much more opportunity for exercise on account of the park, and that we played games even harder, if possible, as here we had three very good tennis courts. . . . The commandant did everything he could to alleviate our hard lot and took particular interest in our games.

The officer who wrote this account was a naval airman named Gunther Plüschow, who on the outbreak of war had been stationed at Kiao-Chau in China. When the German garrison there was besieged in November 1914 he flew out and, after a series of extraordinary adventures, reached the United States, where he took ship for Germany from New York in January 1915, disguised as a Swiss citizen. However, when the vessel – which was Italian – docked at Gibralter, Plüschow was identified and arrested by the British authorities and brought to England as a prisoner of war.

He was first of all imprisoned at Dorchester, of whose staff he wrote: 'There was not a single contemptuous gesture, and never a word of abuse. The prisoners were very contented, the food was good and plentiful, the treatment could not be complained of, and there were plenty of opportunities for games.' He was then transferred to Holyport, where his one complaint was a lack of liberty:

> A number of good books, our string quartet, and a choir, which we had got up ourselves, contributed materially to our social life. We used to rag a great deal, too, and sometimes, when we had had a really good laugh once in a way, we seemed to breathe more freely, and for a short time the dreadful weight of captivity seemed to lift from our shoulders.

Plüschow was moved to Donington Hall, where his stay was short-lived. In July 1915, together with another naval officer, *Oberleutnant* Trefftz, who knew England and spoke English very well, he escaped. To avoid the evening roll-call the two reported sick, and, having arranged with two other prisoners to take their places in bed, they avoided the sentries and hid in the shrubbery near the perimeter wire. At 11 p.m. (on 4 July) they heard a rousing cheer from the barracks; it was the signal that all was clear. Plüschow goes on:

> When we reached the fence, I gave Trefftz my final instructions and handed him my small bundle. I was the first to climb over the fence, which was about nine feet high, and every eight inches the wire was covered with long spikes. Wires charged with electricity were placed two and a half feet from the ground. A mere touch would have sufficed to set in motion a system of bells that would, of course, have given the alarm to the whole camp. We wore leather leggings as protection against the spikes; round our knees we had wound puttees, and we wore leather gloves.
>
> I easily swung myself over the first fence. Trefftz handed over our two bundles and followed me with equal ease. Next we were

143

confronted by a wire obstacle, three feet high by thirty feet wide, contrived according to the latest and most cunning devices. We ran over it like cats. After this we again came to a high barbed wire hedge, built on exactly the same lines as the first and also electrically charged. We managed this, too, except that I tore a piece out of the seat of my trousers, which I had to retrieve, in order to put it in again later.

But, thank God, we were over the boundary! Trefftz and I clasped hands and looked at each other in silence.

The two men, having put on civilian mackintoshes, reached the outskirts of Derby early in the morning and separated at the railway station. Plüschow bought a third-class return ticket to Leicester, where he left the train and boarded another for London. The idea was that he and Trefftz were to rendezvous on the steps of St Paul's Cathedral on the following evening, but Trefftz did not appear and Plüschow learned later that his companion had been arrested at Millwall Docks, presumably while making a reconnaissance of the area.

The next day, after sleeping rough in a garden near Hyde Park, Plüschow was dismayed to find that details of his escape, together with a physical description, had been circulated in the London newspapers and on large posters prominently displayed in the Strand. He was described as being particularly smart and dapper in appearance, so he decided to take immediate steps to change his civilian disguise.

First, I had to get rid of my mackintosh. I therefore went to Blackfriars Station and left my overcoat in the cloakroom. As I handed the garment over the clerk suddenly asked me: 'What is your name, sir?'

The question absolutely bowled me over, as I was quite unprepared for it. With shaking knees I asked: 'Meinen?' [mine], answering in German as I naturally presumed that the man had guessed my identity. 'Oh, I see, Mr Mine – M–i–n–e,' and he handed me a receipt in the name of Mr Mine. It was a miracle that this official had not noticed my terror, and I felt particularly uncomfortable when I had to pass the two policemen who stood on guard at the station and who scrutinized me sharply.

I now sought a quiet, solitary spot. My beautiful soft hat fell accidentally into the river from London Bridge; collar and tie followed suit from another spot; a beautiful gilt stud held my green shirt together. After that a mixture of vaseline, boot-black and coal dust turned my blond hair black and greasy; my hands soon looked as if they had never made acquaintance with water; and at last I wallowed in a coal heap until I had turned into a perfect prototype of the dock labourer on strike. . . . For days I loafed around London, my cap set jauntily at the back of my head, my jacket open, showing my blue sweater and its one ornament, the gilt stud, hands in pockets, whistling and spitting, as is the custom of sailors in ports all the world over.

By a sheer stroke of luck, through a careless conversation between two businessmen. Plüschow heard that a Dutch steamer was soon to dock at Tilbury. He discovered that this vessel, the SS *Mecklenburg*, was in fact one of two fast packets – the other being the SS *Princess Juliana* – which alternated in providing a daily mail and passenger service between Tilbury and Flushing. He hurried to Tilbury and, at about four o'clock in the afternoon, saw the *Mecklenburg* drop anchor and make fast to a buoy directly opposite. It should, he thought, be simple enough to swim to the buoy during the night, climb the hawser, creep on deck, and stow away in a lifeboat.

That was the theory; in practice, however, it proved much more complicated, and Plüschow's first attempt met with disaster when, as he tried to enter the river, he sank waist-deep in slimy mud and only just managed to drag himself clear, exhausted, before he slipped under. As he watched the *Mecklenburg* sail away the next morning, he decided that the real answer to his problem was to steal a small boat downstream, and then drift back towards the steamer on the night tide.

He found a boat at Gravesend and slipped away in it, concealing it under a crumbling bridge and then hiding himself among some tall grasses on the river bank to wait for the incoming tide. As he wrote later:

> My patience still had to undergo a severe test. I remained lying in the grass for the next sixteen hours, until, at eight o'clock that night. . . . I again entered the boat. Cautiously I allowed myself to be driven upstream by the incoming tide, and fastened my boat to the . . . coal-tender near which I had been stranded the night before. Athwart to me lay the *Princess Juliana* moored to her buoy.

This time there was no mistake. Plüschow drifted over to the buoy and pulled himself on to it, pushing his little boat clear. Then he shinned up the hawser and hauled himself over the rail. After hiding for a while near the windlass, he decided to investigate the rest of the deck in his stockinged feet, and it was then he received an unpleasant surprise.

When I looked down from a corner astern the foredeck to the cargo deck I staggered back suddenly. Breathlessly, but without turning a hair, I remained leaning against the ventilator. Below, on the cargo deck, stood two sentries, who were staring fixedly upwards.

Plüschow froze, hoping for the best. The sentries had not seen him, and after half an hour two stewardesses emerged from below decks and engaged them in conversation. With their attention distracted, Plüschow let himself down to the cargo deck and crawled into a lifeboat, where, completely worn out, he fell into a deep sleep. Blasts on the ship's siren woke him, and he cautiously raised the lifeboat's canvas cover to find that the *Princess Juliana* was entering Flushing harbour. Within twenty-four hours, Plüschow, having slipped ashore unnoticed among the passengers, was on a train bound for Germany.

Kapitänleutnant Gunther Plüschow, who received the Iron Cross (First Class) for his exploit, was one of only four German prisoners of war to escape from Britain during 1914–18; many more got away from the various camps or from working parties, but all were recaptured and were given various periods of detention, with or without hard labour. For example, three Germans were committed for three months to Woking prison on 13 July 1915, for an attempted escape from Leigh camp, while a little later three others were sentenced by a military court at Chester Castle to 84 days' imprisonment, without hard labour, and committed to Chelmsford prison, for attempting to escape from Dyffryn Aled camp near Denbigh. Also in 1915, two German prisoners who escaped from Dorchester camp and who got as far as Hartlepool before being recaptured were given six months' imprisonment, their 'crime' having apparently been compounded by the fact that they were arrested inside a restricted area. These examples serve to show that the Germans were not alone in imposing strict prison sentences on escaping prisoners.

The most determined and persistent escapers were U-boat officers, many of whom were interned in Dyffryn Aled, a camp that boasted double the security measures of most others. There were a number of daring escapes from this camp, and surely the most ambitious and well-planned of all took place in August 1915, when *Korvettenkapitän* Hermann Tholens – who had been First Officer of the light cruiser HIMS *Mainz*, sunk in the Battle of the Heligoland Bight – escaped with two fellow officers, having arranged, through coded messages in letters to Germany, to make rendezvous with a submarine off the Welsh coast. The German Admiralty in fact despatched two boats, the U-38 and U-27; the former was to make the pick-up, with the latter acting as escort and reserve.

The German officers arrived at the rendezvous point at the Great Ormes Head on the night of 14/15 August and, at the appointed time, Tholens flashed a signal by torch. But no submarine appeared, a gale blew up, and in the end the three escapers decided to make their way to Llandudno station, where they hoped to catch a train to London and there get on board a neutral ship. The plan was thwarted by a vigilant police officer, who recognized Tholens and challenged him; the game was up.

Later, it transpired that Tholens and his colleagues had been desperately unlucky. The U-38 had been there all right, but an outcrop of rock had masked Tholen's torch signals. Had this not been so, the German officers would almost certainly have made one of the most dramatic of all 'home runs'.

Apart from the possibility of being taken off by submarine – and this was a very long shot indeed, relying on the most meticulous planning and an enormous amount of luck – the only way home for an escaping German POW was on a neutral vessel, which meant entering a British port. As these were invariably heavily guarded, with stringent security checks, the dangers were obvious – particularly after April 1916, when extra manpower for port and coastal defence was supplied by the newly formed Royal Defence Corps. This worthy organization, the forerunner of the Home Guard in the 1939–45 war, also assumed the responsibility for guard duties at POW camps, which hitherto had been carried out by regular troops on garrison duty. Its colonel-in-chief was the Duke of Connaught, and it was composed mainly of soldiers who had been invalided home from the various battlefronts. As such, they were fully trained fighting men – unlike many of those performing similar duties with their German counterpart, the *Landsturm*. Generally, they were fair in their dealings with prisoners of war, who developed a considerable respect for them.

During 1917, the British government resisted considerable pressure from some sections of the population – particularly those living in coastal areas and London – to house German POWs in areas threatened by enemy bombing raids. In June 1917, there was considerable Press agitation for such a move to take place in the wake of costly raids by Gotha bombers on London and Margate, but it was not until February 1918, when it was established beyond all doubt that British POWs were being drafted to areas under threat of Allied air attack, that similar steps were taken with regard to German prisoners. By May 1918, considerable numbers of German officers were established in requisitioned schools and other buildings at Ramsgate, Margate, and Southend; some of these buildings had been used as temporary hospitals for British and Dominion sick and wounded soldiers, who were now moved to safer locations inland.

There was no prospect of early repatriation for the German prisoners of war once the Armistice had been signed. A state of war still existed between the Allies and Germany, and it was stipulated that the repatriation of German, Austrian, and Hungarian prisoners would only take place after the ratification of the various peace treaties which were being drafted. In November 1918 that was still many months away, and in the mean time the number of German prisoners of war in Britain was swollen by another noteworthy event – the surrender and internment of the German High Seas Fleet.

On 21 November 1918 – the day that the first ship-loads of British prisoners left German ports *en route* for England – the main instalment of the High Seas Fleet under Rear-Admiral Ludwig von Reuter surrendered to Admiral Beatty off the Firth of Forth and sailed on to internment at Scapa Flow. It comprised nine battle-ships, five battle-cruisers, seven light cruisers, and forty-nine destroyers. Later, dozens of U-boats and their crews would also surrender. The latter went to existing POW camps, while the warships at Scapa Flow remained under the care of skeleton crews totalling 1,800 men, the other personnel having also been sent ashore.

The High Seas Fleet stayed in the barren fastness of the Orkneys while the Allies tried to thrash out peace terms with a Germany which, peculiarly, did not consider herself defeated. The months dragged by, and in May 1919 there was grave doubt that the Treaty of Versailles would be ratified by any of the nations represented. On the seventy interned warships, the morale of the crews sank lower; their lot was far worse than that of their colleagues in prison camp; they were forbidden to go ashore and could not even keep in touch with the outside world by radio, for all transmitting and receiving equipment had been removed along with the breech blocks and rangefinders of the guns. For food and newspapers, the officers and men were dependent on the weekly steamer from Wilhelmshaven, although sometimes the captain of the water barge from Kirkwall tossed them copies of the English newspapers. There were no 'extras' from the inhabitants of the Orkneys; too many men had sailed to do battle from that part of the world, and had never returned.

In June 1919, as the peace talks dragged on, the crews of the ships began to be haunted by fears that the former belligerents might soon be at each other's throats again. If that happened, the warships in which they were imprisoned might well be impressed into service with the Royal Navy, a possibility that became increasingly unthinkable to Admiral von Reuter and his officers.

On 21 June, von Reuter sent out the order for the interned warships to be scuttled. Two hours later, in an act of naval suicide unprecedented in history, all seventy ships had gone to the bottom. The Royal Navy's reaction swung between complete calm and almost blind panic, as was later recorded by *Kapitän* Hermann Cordes, in charge of the destroyers.

The orders to hoist the white flag in the event of attack, direct or passive, from land or sea would be meticulously followed. However, we had little chance even to show our flags of surrender. In panicky haste, steam drifters, which had been at anchor beside the mother ships HMS *Sandhurst* and *Victorious*, joined by other armed fishing boats, tugs, salvage vessels and two destroyers, the *Vespa* and *Vega* – which cast off moorings in foaming fury – converged on the unarmed lifeboats, firing at us with cannon, machine guns, and even pistols. They scorned all international law, to say nothing of the dictates of humanity. . . . The English Navy behaved as though insane. . . . There was no explanation for such conduct. They shot wild, boarded one boat only to turn it adrift in the next moment. Some even boarded our sinking ships to snatch our flags and trample upon them, or to gather up souvenirs in the final seconds before the craft submerged. Three of our lifeboats were sunk by gunfire. The shooting kept up even after the survivors had plunged into the water. A half-sunk torpedo boat next came under concentrated fire. Those remaining on board did not know whether to follow their shipmates into the numbing cold of Scapa Flow, in which already floated our dead.

When the mayhem was over six Germans were officially listed as killed, and ten wounded. But many more – and the number remains undisclosed to this day – were 'missing'.

The survivors, after being herded ashore with scant ceremony, were sent to various prison camps. They were still there on 10 January 1920, when the ratification of the peace treaty with Germany was formally signed in Paris. Then the great drift home began, to a Germany devastated by a collapsed economy and war reparations, a Germany wallowing in the bitterness of defeat and divided by political rifts.

Many of the returning prisoners would try to take up the threads of their lives on the land and in the cities; still others would adhere to Germany's armed forces, emasculated by the Treaty of Versailles. And there were those who, in the fullness of time, would rally to a new leader whose promise was to wipe the shame of 1918 from Germany's history.

EPILOGUE
Conscience

In November 1918, just before their repatriation, many British prisoners of war received a short pamphlet from the German Republicans. Printed in English, it was entitled 'A Parting Word'. This is its text.

Gentlemen: The war is over. A little while, and you will see your native land again, your homes, your loved ones, your friends. You will once more take on your accustomed work.

The fortune of war brought you as prisoners into our hands. You were freed, even against your will, from the fighting, from danger, from death. But the joys of peace could not be yours, for there was no peace. Now peace is coming, and peace means liberty. When you are already reunited with your families, thousands of our countrymen will still be pining in far-off prison camp, their hearts as hungry for home as yours.

You have suffered in confinement, as who would not. It was the fate of every prisoner in every prison camp throughout the world to eat his heart out with longing, to chafe against loss of liberty, to suffer from homesickness, brooding discouragement, blank despair. The days, the weeks, the weary years crept by and there was no end in sight. There were many discomforts, irritations, misunderstandings. Your situation has been a difficult one. Our own has been desperate, our country blockaded, our civil population and army suffering from want of proper sufficient food and materials, the enormous demands made upon our harrassed land from every side. These and many other afflictions made it impossible to do all we would have liked to do. Under the circumstances we did our best to lessen the hardships of your lot, to ensure your comfort, to provide you with pastime, enjoyment, mental and bodily recreation. It is not likely that you will ever know how difficult our circumstances have been.

We know that errors have been committed and that there have been hardships for which the former system has been to blame. There have been wrongs and evils on both sides. We hope that you will always think of that, and be just.

You entered the old empire of Germany. You leave a new Republic – the newest and, as we hope to make it, the freest land in the world. We are sorry that you saw so little of what we were proud of in the former Germany – our arts, our sciences, our model cities, our theatres, schools, industries, social institutions, as well as the beauties of our scenery and the real soul of our people, akin in so many things to your own.

But these things will remain part of the new Germany. Once the barriers of misunderstanding and artificial hatred have fallen, we hope that you will learn to know, in happier times, these grander features of a land whose unwilling guests you have been. A barbed wire enclosure is not the proper point of view from which to survey or judge a great nation.

The war has blinded all nations, but if a true and just peace will result in opening the eyes of the peoples to the fact that their interests are common – that no difference in flags, speech or nationality can alter the truth of the fraternity of all men – this war will not have been fought in vain. If the peoples at last realise that it is not each other who are their enemies, but the ruthless forces of imperialism and capitalism, of militarism of all sorts, of jingo-journalism that sows falsehood, hatred and suspicion, then this war will not have been fought in vain. Then peace will not be established in vain.

We hope that every one of you will go home carrying a message of goodwill, conciliation and enlightenment. Let all men in our new epoch go forth as missionaries of the new evangel, as interpreters between nation and nation.

The valiant dead who once fought against each other have long been sleeping as comrades side by side in the earth. May the living who once fought against each other labour as comrades side by side upon this self-same earth.

That is the message with which we bid you farewell.

EPILOGUE

One of these pamphlets is today lodged in the archives of the Imperial War Museum, London. Thousands more, within minutes or hours of their receipt, were put to the traditional use which soldiers the world over find for conveniently sized scraps of paper.

APPENDIX
PRINCIPAL POW CAMPS IN
GERMANY, 1914–18

ALTMARK

Gardelegen
Hagen Berge
Stendal

BADEN

Baden
Constanz
Freiburg
Heidelberg
Heuberg
Karlsruhe
Mannheim
Pforzheim
Rastatt
Tauberbischofsheim

BAVARIA

Aschaffenberg
Bayreuth
Eichstätt
Erlangen
Fürstenfeldbrück
Germersheim
Hammelburg
Ingolstadt
Kempten
Landshut
Lechfeld

Nürnburg
Regensburg
Würzburg
Ziefelhutten

BRANDENBURG

Berlin
Blankenburg
Brandenburg
Cottbus
Crossen
Cüstrin
Döberitz
Dyrotz
Frankfurt on Oder
Guben
Havelberg
Karstadt
Merzdorf
Muncheberg
Neuruppin
Ruhleben
Wünsdorf
Zossen

BRUNSWICK

Braunschweig
Holzminden

HANOVER

Bucholz
Edemissen-Strodthagen
Golle
Görden
Göttingen
Hameln
Hann Münden
Hanover
Herrenhausen
Leese
Osnabrück
Poggenmoor
Schwarmstedt
Seesen
Soltau
Stolzenau
Ströhen
Verden
Wahnbeck

HARZ

Altenau
Clausthal
Elbinerode

HESSE

Darmstadt
Frankfurt on Main

Giessen
Griesheim
Kassel
Limburg
Mainz
Niederzwehren
Worms

MECKLENBURG

Boizenberg
Furstenberg
Gorries
Güstrow
Parchim

NEU-BRANDENBURG

Augustabad
Neu Brandenburg

OLDENBURG

Delmenhorst
Oldenburg
Vechta

POMERANIA

Altdamm
Danzig-Troyl
Hamburg
Johannisthal
Lübeck
Stargard
Stralsund

POSEN

Schneidemühl
Skammerschutz

PRUSSIA

Arys
Czersk

Hammerstein
Heilsberg
Preussisch Holland
Stallupönen
Tuchel

RHEINPFALZ

Landau
Ludwigshafen

RHINELAND

Aachen
Bedburg
Crefeld
Duisburg
Dusseldorf
Friedrichsfeld
Hamborn
Jülich
Koblenz
Köln
Mühlheim
Oberhausen
Remscheid
Rheinback
Saarbrücken
Saarlouis
Siegburg
Trier
Wahn

SAXONY

Alten-Grabow
Bad Colberg
Chemnitz
Erfurt
Halle
Königsbrück
Magdeburg
Merseburg
Quedlinburg
Weimar
Wittenberg

Zittau
Zwickau

SCHLESWIG-HOLSTEIN

Heidmühlen
Kiel
Oldesloe
Springhirsch
Wasbeck

SILESIA

Lamsdorf
Lauban
Neisse
Neuhammer
Sagan
Schweidnitz
Sprottau

THURINGIA

Langensalza
Ohrdruf

WESTPHALIA

Bielefeld
Burgsteinfurt
Dortmund
Dülmen
Gütersloh
Meschede
Minden
Münster
Neuenkirchen
Paderborn
Sennelager

WURTTEMBERG

Ludwigsburg
Ost and West
Ravensburg
Stuttgart

SELECT BIBLIOGRAPHY

NARRATIVES CONSULTED IN THE IMPERIAL WAR MUSEUM: PRIMARY SOURCES QUOTED IN TEXT

Anonymous (*Diary of a Prisoner of War*)
Bellamy, R. T., Pte
Blain, W. C., Lt Royal Flying Corps
Brady, J., Cpl King's Own Yorkshire Light Infantry
Byrne, J. A. D., Able Seaman
Champion, H., Capt. Royal Flying Corps
Green, C. E., Cpl Scots Guards
Herd, E., Pte
Jowsey, W., Tpr Royal Horse Artillery
McDaid, J., Pte Argyll and Sutherland Highlanders
McMurtrie, G. D. J., Capt. Somerset Light Infantry
Preston, R., Pte King's Royal Rifle Corps
Rees, H. C., Brig.-Gen. OC 158 Brigade
Speight, A., Cpl Durham Light Infantry

Narrative and report of conditions in Swiss internment camps

PRINCIPAL PUBLISHED SOURCES QUOTED IN TEXT

Bennett, J. B. Sterndale (1939) 'A prisoner's last view of Germany', in *The Great War – I Was There*, Part 47, August, London: Amalgamated Press Ltd.
Brown, Percy (1932) *Round the Corner*, London: Faber & Faber.
Evans, A. J. (1930) *The Escaping Club*, London: The Bodley Head.
Garrett, Richard (1981) *P.O.W.*, London: David & Charles.
Hammerton, Sir, J. A. (1931) *History of the Great War*, London: HMSO.
Hoehling, A. A. (1965) *The Great War at Sea*, London: Arthur Barker.
Joyce, James Avery (1959) *Red Cross International*, London: Hodder & Stoughton.

Keith, A. E. (1939) 'I escaped from Ruhleban,' in *The Great War – I Was There*, Part 32, May, London: Amalgamated Press Ltd.

Lewis, N. (1924) 'I was a prisoner under the sea', *Sunday Graphic*.

Plüschow, G. (1929) *My Escape from Donington Hall*, London: The Bodley Head.

Regimental Journal of the Royal Hampshire Regiment (1920), vol. 15.

Rorie, David (1925) *A Medico's Luck in the War*, Aberdeen: Milne & Hutchinson. (Experiences of Capt. R. Tennant Bruce.)

Spaight, J. M. (1933) *Air Power and War Rights*, London: Longmans, Green & Co.

INDEX